Bodhi Light Tales
Volume ❶

By Venerable Master Hsing Yun

星雲說喻 中英對照版

星雲大師 著

布施 On Generosity

Bodhi Light Tales: Volume 1 / 星雲說喻 中英對照版①
By Venerable Master Hsing Yun
星雲大師 著

Editor-in-Chief: Venerable Miao Guang
主編：妙光法師

Editorial and Translation Committee:
Fo Guang Shan Institute of Humanistic Buddhism, Center of International Affairs
英文編輯/翻譯：財團法人佛光山人間佛教研究院國際中心

Front Cover Illustrator: Venerable Dao Pu
封面繪圖：道璞法師

Illustrators: Venerable Dao Pu and Sedona Garcia
內頁繪圖：道璞法師、Sedona Garcia

Published and Distributed by: Gandha Samudra Culture Co. Ltd.
出版/發行：香海文化事業有限公司
Address: No.117, Section 3, Sanhe Road, Sanchong District, Taiwan R.O.C.
地址：241台灣新北市三重區三和路三段117號6樓
Tel 電話：+886-2-2971-6868
Fax 傳真：+886-2-2971-6577

Price 定價：NTD390 (USD 13)
Published 出版：September 2023/2023年9月

ISBN: 978-626-96782-3-5

人間佛教叢書

星雲說喻 中英對照版①

出版•發行•編製 香海文化事業有限公司

發行人 慈容法師Ⅰ執行長 妙蘊法師Ⅰ編輯部 賴瀅如 蔡惠琪Ⅰ美術設計 許廣僑

香海悅讀網 https://gandhabooks.com Ⅰ電子信箱 gandha@ecp.fgs.org.tw

劃撥帳號 19110467 Ⅰ戶名 香海文化事業有限公司

登 記 證 局版北市業字第1107號

總 經 銷 時報文化出版企業股份有限公司

地址 333桃園縣龜山鄉萬壽路二段351號Ⅰ電話 (02)2306-6842

國家圖書館出版品預行編目(CIP)資料

星雲說喻1,Bodhi Light Tales Volume I,
星雲大師(Venerable Master Hsing Yun)作.
-- 新北市 : 香海文化事業有限公司, 2023.09
232面;27.9 X 21公分
中英對照版
ISBN 978-626-96782-3-5(精裝)

224.519   112012188

f 香海文化 Q   香海悅讀網

Bodhi Light Tales

Volume ①

Stories

Biography of Venerable Master Hsing Yun

Venerable Master Hsing Yun was born in 1927 in Jiangdu, Jiangsu Province, China. At the age of 12, he was tonsured by Venerable Master Zhikai in Qixia Temple, Nanjing, with Dajue Temple in Yixing, Jiangsu, as his ancestral temple. He later became the 48th-generation lineage holder of the Linji Chan school. In 1947, he graduated from Jiaoshan Buddhist College, and also trained at various Chan, Pure Land, and Vinaya monasteries, including Jinshan, Qixia, and others. He received a comprehensive Buddhist education in the lineage, teachings, and Vinaya disciplines. Later on, the Venerable Master was invited to serve as the principal of Baita Elementary School, and also the editor-in-chief of *Raging Billows Monthly*.

In the spring of 1949, the Venerable Master arrived in Taiwan. He served as the editor-in-chief of *Human Life Magazine*, *Buddhism Today Magazine*, and *Awakening the World*.

In 1967, the Venerable Master founded the Fo Guang Shan Buddhist Order, with the Four Objectives: to propagate the Dharma through culture; to foster talents through education; to benefit society through charity, and to purify people's minds through spiritual cultivation. Guided by the principles of Humanistic Buddhism, he went on to establish over three hundred temples worldwide. Additionally, he oversaw the creation of various art galleries, libraries, publishing companies, bookstores, the *Merit Times* newspaper, and the Cloud and Water Mobile Clinic. Furthermore, he established sixteen Buddhist colleges and founded three high schools and five universities, including the University of the West in the United States, Fo Guang University in Taiwan, Nanhua University in Taiwan, Nan Tien Institute in Australia, and Guang Ming College in the Philippines. Notably, he also established the Institute of Humanistic Buddhism.

In 1970, the Venerable Master established Da Ci Children's Home and the Lanyang Ren Ai Senior Citizen's Home, providing shelter and care for vulnerable young children, and elderly individuals. He also actively engaged in emergency relief efforts, contributing to the fostering of a welfare society. Then, in 1991, he founded the Buddha's Light International Association (BLIA) and was elected as the President of the World Headquarters. Under his guidance, the association's mission expanded, symbolized by the saying, "the Buddha's Light shining over three thousand realms, and the Dharma water flowing continuously through the five continents."

In 1977, the *Fo Guang Buddhist Canon*, the *Fo Guang Dictionary of Buddhism*, and the 132-volume *Selected Chinese Buddhist Texts in Modern Language* were compiled. In 2017, the *Complete Works of Venerable Master Hsing Yun* was published, comprising 365 volumes with over 30 million words, systematically expounding the ideologies, teachings, theories, and practical outcomes of Humanistic Buddhism.

In 2023, the Venerable Master peacefully passed away, his virtuous deeds complete and fulfilled, having reached the age of ninety-seven. He was revered as the Founding Master of the Fo Guang Order, and he left behind this poignant poem:

A mind with the compassionate vow to deliver sentient beings,

A body like a boat on the Dharma ocean, unbound.

Should you ask what I have achieved in this lifetime?

Peace and happiness shine upon the five continents.

星雲大師簡介

　　星雲大師，江蘇江都人，一九二七年生，十二歲禮志開上人為師，祖庭江蘇宜興大覺寺，傳臨濟正宗第四十八世。一九四七年於焦山佛學院畢業，期間曾參學金山、棲霞等禪淨律學諸大叢林，歷經宗下、教下、律下等完整的佛門教育。之後應聘為白塔國小校長，主編《怒濤》月刊。

　　一九四九年春來臺，主編《人生雜誌》、《今日佛教》、《覺世》等佛教刊物。

　　一九六七年創建佛光山，樹立「以文化弘揚佛法，以教育培養人才，以慈善福利社會，以共修淨化人心」四大弘法宗旨，以「人間佛教」為宗風，先後在世界各地創建三百餘所道場，創辦多所美術館、圖書館、出版社、書局、人間福報、雲水醫院，興辦佛教學院十六所，中學三所，及西來、南華、佛光、南天、光明五所大學，及人間佛教研究院。

　　一九七○年後，相繼成立「大慈育幼院」、「仁愛之家」，收容撫育無依之幼童、老人及從事急難救濟等福利社會。一九九一年成立「國際佛光會」，被推為總會會長，實踐「佛光普照三千界，法水長流五大洲」的理想。

　　一九七七年編纂《佛光大藏經》、《佛光大辭典》、《中國佛教經典寶藏精選白話版》等。二○一七年出版《星雲大師全集》，共三百六十五冊，三千餘萬字，有系統地闡述人間佛教的思想、學說、理論，以及實踐結果。

　　二○二三年，大師住世緣盡，淨業圓滿，享耆壽九十七，被奉為佛光堂上第一代開山祖師，留遺偈：「心懷度眾慈悲願，身似法海不繫舟，問我一生何所求，平安幸福照五洲」。

Editor's Introduction

Bodhi Light Tales is a captivating 6-volume collection of stories focused on the Six Paramitas, narrated by the revered Venerable Master Hsing Yun. Originally published in Chinese as *Xingyun shuoyu* (星雲說喻), these Buddhist Tales by Venerable Master Hsing Yun emerged from his enlightening talks and lectures on Humanistic Buddhism. In 2019, we took the initiative to adapt these stories into English as an ongoing audiobook series for the Bodhi Light Tales Anchor Podcast channel. However, our ultimate vision has always been to present them in a book format. As the original stories were concise and lacked additional details, the English adaptations were intentionally modified from the Chinese. In essence, the English tales are not direct translations of their original Chinese counterparts. To ensure that readers of all ages, faiths, beliefs, and cultures can connect with these stories, we employed several key approaches during the transition from Chinese to English, which we will elaborate on below.

To make the main characters more relatable, we added background information such as their names, occupations, and personalities. Thorough research was conducted to maintain historical and factual accuracy. We hope this additional information will help readers delve deeper into their favorite characters and even encourage further exploration.

Furthermore, we made certain adaptations to account for cultural differences. For instance, in one of the stories, using chopsticks was originally

featured, but we replaced it with forks in the English version to resonate with English-speaking readers. Similarly, silk brocade bags known as *"jin nang"* (錦囊) in the original tales were transformed into envelopes. These adjustments were made to ensure that the stories remain relatable to English readers.

Each tale concludes with a summary of its morals, providing readers with a clear understanding of the story's meaning and key lessons. These summaries highlight challenges people face in today's world and offer practical applications for daily life.

Additionally, we included Dharma Words from Venerable Master Hsing Yun at the end of each story, offering readers a final nugget of wisdom to take away. These quotes were carefully selected based on their relevance to the moral of each story. Venerable Master Hsing Yun originally shared these words of encouragement and advice based on his life experiences, aiming to inspire mindfulness and guide individuals in times of uncertainty.

Remember, Buddha-nature resides within all of us, regardless of whether we practice Buddhism or not. Both children and adults have the power to better themselves and positively impact the world around them. Our sincere hope is that these stories will inspire people of all ages, instilling in them a sense of inspiration, courage, and compassion. May this collection serve as a source of inspiration as you navigate through life's journey toward self-awakening!

編者序

《星雲說喻　中英對照版》，是一套引人入勝的六冊選集，收編了一百二十篇由敬愛的星雲大師講說，以六度波羅蜜為主題的故事。這些故事最初收錄在《星雲說喻》，大師喜歡在演講中穿插生動有趣的故事，以傳遞人間佛教思想與實踐的精髓。

2019年，我們首次將《星雲說喻》的內容翻譯成有聲故事書，並於 Anchor 播客平台推出「菩提心燈」系列故事 (Bodhi Light Tales Podcast)。這些年，我們一直期待著將這些故事結集成冊，如今因緣條件具足，並以中英雙語圖書的形式呈現。為了讓來自各年齡層、宗教、信仰，以及文化的讀者皆能與故事產生共鳴，我們在精簡扼要的原文基礎上發揮想像，增添了一些原文故事沒有的情節。也就是說，這套故事書中的英文故事是經過編譯的創作，非中文的直譯對照。編譯的幾項原則要點說明如下：

首先是對故事人物的背景資訊加以補充，如：名字、所從事行業，及個性等。我們蒐集文獻和查證史料，以確保人物的歷史背景正確無誤。希望藉由建構鮮明的人物特性，能帶給

讀者更多親和力，也鼓勵讀者進一步探索喜愛的角色。

第二，調整文化差異的部分。例如，有一篇以「筷子」為特寫的故事，在編譯成英文時，我們將它改成「叉子」；再如，古代用來收納貴重物品的「錦囊」，在英文故事中則改以「信封」來呈現。以上改編目的，是為了加強故事元素與西方讀者日常生活之間的經驗連結。

第三，提綱挈領出每篇故事的主旨和寓意，讓讀者更容易把握住故事所要傳達的信息，引導省思。同時，也探討人們在現當代可能面臨的挑戰，幫助讀者連結所學，實際應用在日常生活之中。

故事結束，為每篇故事搭配一則精選「星雲法語」，作為總結故事核心寓意的智慧錦囊。「星雲法語」原是大師依據自己的人生經歷寫下的鼓勵和箴言，期望藉此帶給大家正念，在人生迷茫處作一盞指引方向的明燈。

學佛與否，佛性本自具足。無論是兒童還是成人，我們都有能力讓自己和周遭的世界變得更好、更正向。希望這套故事書能啟迪心性，讓各個年齡層的讀者在邁向自我覺醒的生命旅程中，充滿能量、勇氣和慈悲。

How to Use This Book

如何使用本書

Bodhi Light Tales by Venerable Master Hsing Yun are selected stories on the Six Paramitas: Generosity, Precept, Patience, Diligence, Meditative Concentration, and Wisdom. These short stories, in a 6-volume set, offer readers opportunities to contemplate the Buddha's teachings and concepts of Humanistic Buddhism.

星雲大師著《星雲說喻 中英對照版》收錄120篇精選故事,以六度波羅蜜為主題:布施、持戒、忍辱、精進、禪定、般若。此系列共有6冊,讓讀者有機會透過故事思維佛陀的教義和人間佛教的理念。

Title Page 篇章頁

1. Category
one of the Six Paramitas

類別六度波羅蜜之一

2. Story Title
in English and Chinese

中英文故事篇名

3. QR Code to Audio
a. Scan the QR code
b. Scroll down to find story title
c. Press ▶ to listen

掃碼聽故事
a. 掃描二維碼
b. 點選故事
c. ▶ 播放與聆聽故事

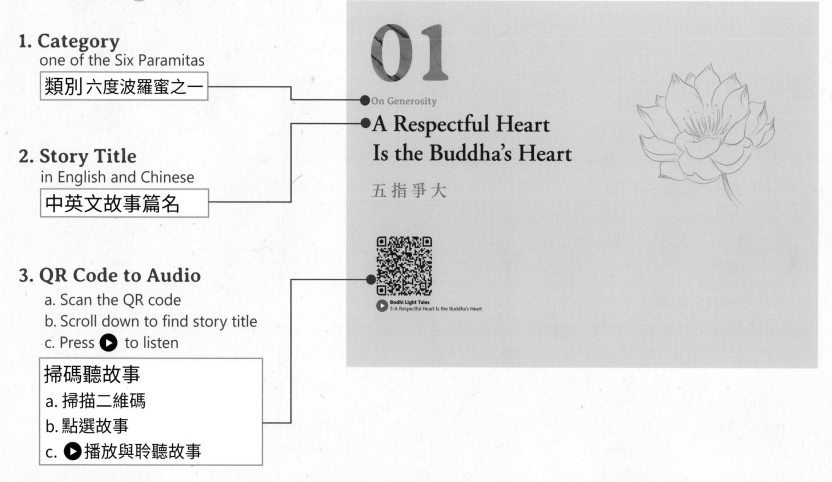

01

On Generosity

A Respectful Heart
Is the Buddha's Heart

五指爭大

Bodhi Light Tales
3-A Respectful Heart Is the Buddha's Heart

Story Pages 故事內容

Scan me to listen!
掃我，聆聽故事！

4. Illustration

繪圖

5. Story (in English)

English adaptation

英文故事

6. Story (in Chinese)

Original content, as told by Venerable Master Hsing Yun

中文故事

7. Vocabulary List

English keywords with Chinese definitions
to guide bilingual readers

詞彙表
英文關鍵詞彙及其中文解釋，
為雙語讀者提供輔助閱讀資源。

One day, the five fingers of a hand were having a chat, and one of them asked, "Of the five of us, who is the leader?"

The Thumb was the first to answer, "Of course I am the leader, because when people give a signal[1] of approval[2] to what is good or best, they would put me up and hide the rest of you in a fist. That is also why a "thumbs up" is given to what people approve of. So of course, I am the leader!" said the Thumb proudly.

The Index Finger was not convinced[3], "If someone wants to get people's attention, they don't stick out their thumb, do they? No, they raise me. And, when it comes to tasting food - which finger do they use to dab[4] the bowl or the dish for a delicious taste? Me! Without me, you would never know what good food is. Without me, you could end up with bad food. That is why I'm the leader. I am vital[5] to your survival."

The Middle Finger laughed and said, "Look,

VOCABULARY

1. signal (n.) 信號；暗號
2. approval (n.) 批准；認可
3. convinced (adj.) 確信的；信服的
4. dab (v.) 輕觸；輕擦
5. vital (adj.) 必不可少的；極其重要的

有一天，五根手指頭召開小組會議，彼此爭相做老大。首先，大拇指威風凜凜地說：「我是老大！只要我大拇指豎起來，就是最大、最好的象徵。所以，你們都要聽我的！」

食指聽了不服氣，反駁說：「民以食為天，人類品嘗美味的時候，都是先用我嘗味道的。尤其我還是一個指揮，只要我的手比向東，人們就往東；比向西，人們就往西。所以你們都應該聽我的，我最大！」

- 21 -

8. Dharma Words

Quote from Venerable Master Hsing Yun
expressing the heart of each story

星雲大師法語
總結故事的核心價值和寓意

Dharma Words by Venerable Master Hsing Yun

Having roots in your heart, you can blossom and bear fruit;
Having a vow in your heart, you can advance business affairs;
Having reason in your heart, you can travel all over the world;
Having clarity of view in your mind, you can stand true;
Having virtue in your heart, you can tolerate all things;
Having the Way in your heart, you can embrace everything.

星雲大師法語

心中要有根，才能開花結果；心中要有願，才能成就事業；
心中要有理，才能走遍天下；心中要有主，才能立處皆真；
心中要有德，才能涵容萬物；心中要有道，才能擁有一切。

01

On Generosity

A Respectful Heart
Is the Buddha's Heart

五指爭大

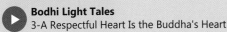

Bodhi Light Tales
3-A Respectful Heart Is the Buddha's Heart

One day, the five fingers of a hand were having a chat, and one of them asked, "Of the five of us, who is the leader?"

The Thumb was the first to answer, "Of course I am the leader, because when people give a signal[1] of approval[2] to what is good or best, they would put me up and hide the rest of you in a fist. That is also why a "thumbs up" is given to what people approve of. So of course, I am the leader!" said the Thumb proudly.

The Index Finger was not convinced[3], "If someone wants to get people's attention, they don't stick out their thumb, do they? No, they raise me. And, when it comes to tasting food, which finger do they use to dab[4] the bowl or the dish for a delicious taste? Me! Without me, you would never know what good food is. Without me, you could end up with bad food. That is why I'm the leader. I am vital[5] to your survival."

The Middle Finger laughed and said, "Look,

VOCABULARY

1. signal (n.) 信號；暗號
2. approval (n.) 批准；認可
3. convinced (adj.) 確信的；信服的
4. dab (v.) 輕觸；輕擦
5. vital (adj.) 必不可少的；極其重要的

　　有一天，五根手指頭召開小組會議，彼此爭相做老大。首先，大拇指威風凜凜地說：「我是老大！只要我大拇指豎起來，就是最大、最好的象徵。所以，你們都要聽我的！」

　　食指聽了不服氣，反駁說：「民以食為天，人類品嘗美味的時候，都是先用我嘗味道的。尤其我還是一個指揮，只要我的手比向東，人們就往東；比向西，人們就往西。所以你們都應該聽我的，我最大！」

I am in the middle, I am the tallest and so the biggest. By virtue[6] of my size alone, you should listen to me, and this means I should be the leader."

The Ring Finger smiled gently, "You all make good points. But you forget that when people get married, they slip[7] the wedding ring on me. So I am clearly the most important. I am the one who gets all the diamond rings and jewelry. This means I am the most valuable among you all, and that is why I am the leader. How can you others compare[8]?" concluded the Ring Finger.

The Thumb and the three fingers continued to argue[9], each thinking they were the greatest, and therefore the rightful leader.

After a while, they turned to the Little Finger, who had not said a word throughout the conversation, "You've been awfully[10] quiet. Who do you think is the greatest among us and

VOCABULARY

6. virtue (n.) 美德
7. slip (v.) 迅速地做；悄悄地做
8. compare (v.) 對比；比較
9. argue (v.) 爭論；爭吵
10. awfully (adv.) 非常；極其

隨後，中指不可一世地說：「在五根手指當中，我居中、我最長，你們都應該聽命於我才對！」

優雅的無名指接著就說：「我雖然叫無名指，但是你們看！一般人過生日、做壽、結婚時配戴的金戒指、鑽石戒指，都是套在我的身上，只有我全身珠光寶氣。我這個無名指才是真正有名啊！」

therefore the leader of the hand? Who do you think should be the boss?"

The Little Finger looked at them all in turn and said quietly, "Well, I am the smallest finger, few people put rings on me, or hold me in the air or use me to taste food, and no one uses me in a gesture[11] of approval. Also, I am the last finger. So, I would not dare[12] to compare myself with any of you."

Just as the other fingers gloated[13] in satisfaction over the Little Finger's reply, it continued, "However, when people join their palms and bow[14] to the Buddha and the Sages, I am the closest." Then, the other fingers and the thumb nodded[15] quietly and wasted no more time on this question.

VOCABULARY

11. gesture (n.) 手勢
12. dare (v.) 敢於；膽敢
13. gloated (v.) 獨自暗笑
14. bow (v.) 鞠躬
15. nodded (v.) 點頭；(尤指)點頭贊同

四根手指各自炫耀了自己的偉大及重要性之後，唯獨小指頭默然不語。大家就問：「咦！小拇指，你怎麼不說話呢？」

小拇指說：「我最小、最後，怎麼能跟你們相比呢？」正當大家讚歎小拇指的謙虛的時候，小拇指接著又說：「不過，當我們合掌禮敬師長、佛祖、聖賢的時候，可是我最靠近他們喔。」

In life, we often see people competing to be the leader. Some will point to their status[16], wealth, or beauty as to why they should be the leader.

However, status, power, or position are not the real qualities of leadership or even necessarily the signs of the best leader.

What makes a person stand out as a leader is how they treat and deal with others. Do they act with patience[17] and compassion? Do they respect and consider others?

If your heart is big enough to embrace[18] all members of your family, you are capable[19] of being the head of the family.

If your heart is big enough to accept a city and all its people, then you have the ability to be its mayor.

If your heart is big enough to carry all the people of your country, and you act with consideration[20] and compassion for all the citizens, then you are capable of

VOCABULARY

16. status (n.) 地位
17. patience (n.) 忍耐
18. embrace (v.) 擁抱
19. capable (adj.) 有能力的
20. consideration (n.) 體貼；關心

社會上爭做老大的人，屢見不鮮。但是真正的老大，並不是用身分的高低、排名的先後去衡量的，誰能對人慈悲、友愛、服務、謙虛、恭敬，誰就是最大。

becoming the president or the leader.

If your heart can accept and encompass[21] the Earth or even the entire Three Thousand Realms[22], then your heart will be in perfect harmony with the Buddha's heart.

Just remember, every noble[23] and respected person started from humble[24] beginnings.

A respectful[25] heart is the Buddha's Heart.

VOCABULARY

21. encompass (v.) 包含
22. Three Thousand Realms (n.) 三千世界
23. noble (adj.) 高尚的；偉大的；崇高的
24. humble (adj.) 謙遜的
25. respectful (adj.) 表示尊敬的；尊重的

　　所以，偉大不是爭取來的，而是一個人表現出來的氣度。你的心能包容一個家庭，你就可以做家長；你的心能包容一個城市，你就可以做市長；你的心能包容一個國家，你就可以做總統、領袖；你的心能包容一個地球，乃至三千法界，你就可以和佛心契合無間了。

Dharma Words by Venerable Master Hsing Yun

Having roots in your heart, you can blossom and bear fruit;
Having a vow in your heart, you can advance business affairs;
Having reason in your heart, you can travel all over the world;
Having clarity of view in your mind, you can stand true;
Having virtue in your heart, you can tolerate all things;
Having the Way in your heart, you can embrace everything.

星雲大師法語

心中要有根，才能開花結果；心中要有願，才能成就事業；
心中要有理，才能走遍天下；心中要有主，才能立處皆真；
心中要有德，才能涵容萬物；心中要有道，才能擁有一切。

notes

02

On Generosity

Compassion Is Like a Bridge

慈悲如橋

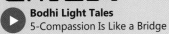

Bodhi Light Tales
5-Compassion Is Like a Bridge

Once upon a time, a young man named Ralph, went to the temple to seek advice from a Buddhist monk. Ralph was having problems at work. He couldn't relate[1] to his colleagues and was wondering if he should just simply quit[2].

He said to the monk, "Master, I just started this job and I already hate it. I can't relate to anyone at work because I find it so hard to communicate[3] with them. I want to quit but this would be the third job I quit this month!"

The monk looked at Ralph and asked, "Last time you were here, you mentioned that you rescued[4] an injured[5] dog you found by the roadside. Can you tell me again how you rescued him?"

Remembering the dog, Ralph's face lit up and he retold the rescue, "Well I was walking home, and it was raining. I saw the puppy, he

---

VOCABULARY

1.　relate (v.) 產生共鳴
2.　quit (v.) 離開；辭職；放棄
3.　communicate (v.) 溝通
4.　rescued (v.) 解救；救出
5.　injured (adj.) 受傷的

有一次，一位信徒帶著她的孩子上山來找法師，請求協助。原來是她的孩子，今年剛從學校畢業，進入社會工作。可是，才做沒多久，就想要換工作，問其原因，兒子滿臉痛苦地對媽媽說：「辦公室裡的人，實在很難溝通。」

憂心的母親掛念兒子的前程，心想：「如果第一關都不能突破，將來人生旅程的挫折還很多，他要怎麼面對？總不能一年到頭都在換工作啊！」這位信徒便請師父幫忙，看看有沒有辦法可以讓孩子和同事溝通？

looked weak, injured, and was just lying on the side of the road. I couldn't just leave it there, so I brought it home. And fed it and treated its injuries."

The monk asked, "How's the dog doing now?"

Ralph, still smiling, continued, "He's completely healed[6] and healthy now! I decided to keep him, and named him Einstein because he is very smart. Well, Einstein is a great dog. When I come home from work, and he hears the door, he would fetch[7] me my slippers[8]!"

The monk smiled and said, "What a nice thing to do."

Ralph, now beaming[9] with joy, added, "Whenever the phone rings, Einstein nudges[10] me nonstop till I pick it up! He lies by my side as I read at night, and wakes me up when my alarm

VOCABULARY

6. healed (v.) 痊癒
7. fetch (v.) 取來
8. slippers (n.) 拖鞋
9. beaming (v.) 微笑
10. nudges (v.) 輕推

師父對這男孩說：「我記得你家裡好像養了一隻小狗？」

他很得意回答：「是啊，那是我養的。」

師父又問：「這條狗是怎麼來的？」

「哦，那是在一個下雨的夜裡，我走在回家的路上，忽然看到一隻受傷的小狗，躺在路邊淋雨，心中十分不忍，於是就把牠帶回來飼養。後來，牠的傷好了，也不離開，就住下來。這條狗十分善解人意，當我回到

goes off in the morning. I have never met such a wonderful dog! He's my new best friend."

Sensing Ralph's joy at talking about his dog, the Monk replied, "Sounds like you two get along really well."

Ralph nodded[11] in reply, "Yes of course. We have a great connection[12]. We communicate all the time. We understand each other. And we love each other."

The monk looked at Ralph and asked, "That's right. But, let me ask you something. Humans and dogs don't speak the same language. Have you ever wondered[13] why you can communicate with your dog? Do you know why you get along so well?"

Ralph, puzzled[14], shaking his head, admitted[15], "Actually Master, I never really thought about it. Do you know why?"

VOCABULARY

11. nodded (v.) 點頭
12. connection (n.) 聯繫
13. wondered (v.) 疑惑；想知道
14. puzzled (adj.) 迷惑的；感到不解的
15. admitted (v.) 承認

家，牠就會咬拖鞋來給我穿，甚至我在房間裡，客廳的電話響了，牠也會跑來咬我的衣服，叫我去接電話。這條狗是這麼聰明又善解人意，我實在很喜歡牠。」

看著這個年輕孩子，眉飛色舞地談起這隻狗，法師就說：「那你和這條狗一定很能處得來。」

「是啊，是啊，因為我們能溝通啊！牠都能了解我的意思，所以我也很喜歡牠。」

The monk nodded, and said, "It is because, from the very beginning, you were compassionate[16] towards him. Although you and your dog are different in many ways, you get along[17] because you love him very much. Keeping that in mind, if you treat[18] your colleagues with the same compassion and kindness[19], then communicating with them isn't difficult. Compassion is like a bridge between people. It connects them and brings them closer together. Why don't you give your job a second chance? See if things change for the better?"

Ralph smiled and was filled with joy at hearing the Monk's advice, "Thank you for your compassion, Master!"

With a compassionate heart, Ralph went back to work and found a way to get along with his coworkers[20].

VOCABULARY

16. compassionate (adj.) 慈悲的
17. get along (phrase) 相處融洽；和睦相處
18. treat (v.) 對待
19. kindness (n.) 仁慈
20. coworkers (n.) 同事

「這就對了，為什麼你能夠和牠溝通？為什麼你們能夠融洽相處？這是因為一開始你就以慈悲心接納牠。所以，雖然人和狗的形體不同、語言不同、動作不同，可是你們還是可以溝通、相處，而且你也很愛護牠呀！」

法師接著又說：「同樣的道理，假如我們對辦公室裡的人，也能夠以一顆慈悲心、愛心，來和他們相處，這樣一來要不溝通也難。再說，人跟狗之間，沒有共同的語言，都能夠溝通了，為什麼人與人之間有了共

The moral[21] of this story is, if we face each day with compassion and loving-kindness[22], we shall bring happiness and inspiration[23] to others. With a compassionate[24] heart, we can go anywhere for it is like a bridge that brings people together. And with compassion, we will always have friends wherever[25] we go.

VOCABULARY

21. moral (n.) 寓意
22. loving-kindness (n.) 慈愛；悲心
23. inspiration (n.) 靈感；啟發
24. compassionate (adj.) 慈悲的
25. wherever (adv.) 無論到哪裡

同的肢體、語言、生活方式、起居作息，反而不能溝通呢？因此，如果我們能夠以慈悲心為出發點，來接納別人，溝通不良的狀況自然會減少。回去以後，你不妨試試看！」

慈悲就如一座橋樑，人際間藉著它來達到溝通順暢。如果我們每天都能心存慈悲地出門，那麼無論行到何處，都會有讓人歡喜、如沐春風的感覺，自然通行無礙。

Dharma Words by Venerable Master Hsing Yun

Use a kind, compassionate heart to care for all living beings;
Use kind, compassionate eyes to look at all things;
Use kind, compassionate words to rejoice in and praise others;
Use kind, compassionate hands to do good deeds broadly.

星雲大師法語

用慈悲的心靈關懷眾生，用慈悲的眼神看待萬物，
用慈悲的話語隨喜讚歎，用慈悲的雙手廣做好事。

notes

03

On Generosity

Jealousy, Thy Name Is Weakness

師父的腿子

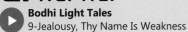

Bodhi Light Tales
9-Jealousy, Thy Name Is Weakness

Once upon a time, there was a compassionate old monk. He was much loved by his disciples who always competed for his attention and affection[1]. But the old monk was wise. He never played favorites among them and made sure he treated all equally.

As the years passed, the old monk suffered constant severe pain due to arthritis[2], his legs hurting most of all. To show their gratitude[3] and devotion[4] to their teacher, the disciples would take turns to massage his legs every day. The senior disciple would massage his right leg, while the junior disciple, the left. Both disciples showed great mindfulness[5] and care at their task. And greatly relieved of his pain, the old monk was most thankful to both of them.

When the senior disciple massaged the Master's right leg, the Master would then use the opportunity to praise his junior Dharma brother in front of him.

"Did you know that your junior brother has such warm and gentle hands? My left leg is

有一位老和尚患了風濕病，兩條腿痠痛不已，他的兩個徒弟為了表達孝心，每天輪流來替師父按摩，大徒弟按摩右腿，小徒弟按摩左腿。

每次大徒弟來按摩右腿的時候，老和尚總會在他面前讚美小徒弟按摩有方，讓他的左腿減少很多疼痛，大徒弟聽了就不大開心；等到小徒弟來按摩左腿的時候，老和尚也在他面前誇讚大徒弟按摩很用心，讓他的右腿日漸康復，小徒弟聽了也不大高興。

feeling so much better."

Likewise, when the junior disciple massaged the Master's left leg, he would then praise his senior disciple in front of him.

"Did you know that your senior Dharma brother has such skillful hands? My right leg is almost pain-free."

What the old monk had intended to do was to encourage[6] his two disciples to learn from each other. But sadly, both disciples misunderstood their teacher's good intentions[7],

and each thought their master was favoring[8] one over the other.

As the days passed, both disciples began to feel increasingly jealous[9] of each other. One day, while his senior brother was absent[10], the junior disciple then broke the old monk's right leg while he was massaging the left.

"Now, Master will only need to rely on me since the other leg is now broken!" thought the junior foolishly.

When the senior disciple returned and saw

VOCABULARY

6. encourage (v.) 鼓勵
7. intentions (n.) 意圖
8. favoring (v.) 偏愛
9. jealous (adj.) 妒忌的
10. absent (adj.) 不在場的

老和尚原本是一番美意，希望師兄弟彼此勉勵，相互學習。可是兩個徒弟卻誤以為師父讚美對方，就是不歡喜自己，因此妒火中燒。有一天，大徒弟來按摩的時候，趁著小師弟出門辦事，心想：師弟，每次師父都說你按摩得怎麼好、怎麼好，哼！今天趁你不在，我就把你按摩的左腿打斷，讓你明天沒有腿可以按摩。

what had happened, he was furious[11].

"How dare[12] you break Master's right leg? I have worked so hard to relieve his pain."

Wanting revenge[13], the senior then broke his master's left leg too.

From this story, it tells us that jealousy is a double-edged[14] sword. When we use this sword to hurt others, we also hurt ourselves. Both disciples were blinded by jealousy. And they had forgotten their original intention and purpose. Instead, they acted senselessly[15]. And in the end, everyone involved suffered greatly. Many of

VOCABULARY

11. furious (adj.) 極其生氣的

12. dare (v.) 敢於；膽敢；竟敢

13. revenge (n.) 報仇

14. double-edged (adj.) 雙刃的

15. senselessly (adv.) 無理智地；無邏輯地

第二天，師弟回來了，看見自己按摩的左腿被打斷了，不禁怒火攻心，就想：一定是師兄故意跟我搗蛋，把我按摩的左腿打斷了。好！我也要把你按摩的右腿打斷，讓你從今以後沒有腿子可以按摩。

就因為師兄弟兩人之間互相嫉妒，師父的損失可更大了，因為他沒有腿了。

us are just like the two disciples. Over small matters, we would treat each other without kindness, respect, or tolerance[16].

According to the Dharma Words by Venerable Master Hsing Yun,

> Anger and hatred are the root of trouble.
> Gratitude and contentment[17] are the source[18] of happiness.
> A moment of loving-kindness can make all things good;
> A moment of anger can turn all situations evil.

So let us endeavor[19] to:

> Practice to speak a mouthful of good words.
> To do a handful of good deeds.
> To show a face full of smiles.
> And have a heart full of joy.

By conquering[20] jealousy, we will be the master of ourselves and the greatest of friends to others.

VOCABULARY

16. tolerance (n.) 寬容；容忍
17. contentment (n.) 滿足；知足
18. source (n.) 來源
19. endeavor (v.) 努力；盡力
20. conquering (v.) 征服

世間上很多的人事，就是因為大家互不相容、互不尊重，你不希望我好、我不希望你好，為了爭一口閒氣，以致兄弟鬩牆、親人反目、朋友仇視。中華民族的民族性有很多優點，但是不希望人家好，則是一個醜陋的惡習。要知道，我們想要今天的社會更好、家庭更好、人我之間更好，一定要歡喜你好、歡喜他好、歡喜大家好啊！

Dharma Words by Venerable Master Hsing Yun

A moment of loving-kindness can make all things good;
A moment of anger can turn all situations evil.

星雲大師法語

一念之慈，萬物皆善；
一心之瞋，千般為惡。

04

The Four Envelopes

四個錦囊

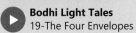

Bodhi Light Tales
19-The Four Envelopes

Once upon a time in a busy town lived a merchant named Michael. Everyone in town knew him. As the days went by, Michael became more and more unhappy. He worried about his company, he worried when he was at home. He even brought his worries to bed. Carrying such burdens[1], he wasn't actually aware of his worries. Though he did not understand why he was so unhappy, he knew he couldn't live this way.

Feeling lost and confused[2], Michael recalled[3] someone sharing about a visit to a monastery for a break. He thought to himself, "I should go and take a look."

When he arrived at the monastery, he went to the Main Shrine[4] where a monk greeted him with joined palms[5].

"What brought you here today?" asked the monk.

Sensing that the monk was friendly, Michael felt comfortable and at ease. So, he began to share his worries and troubles with the monk.

VOCABULARY

1. burdens (n.) 負擔；責任
2. confused (adj.) 困惑的
3. recalled (v.) 回想
4. Main Shrine (n.) 大雄寶殿
5. joined palms (phrase) 合十

有一個生意人，雖然事業做得很大，日子卻過得不快樂，天天煩惱，在工廠裡煩惱，回家也煩惱，就連睡在床上都煩惱不已。究竟是什麼原因，他也無從知道。

就在不知如何是好的情況下，他來到寺院向法師請教。法師說：「我有四個錦囊要給你，每一個錦囊上面都編了號碼，明天早上起來，你按照順序先打開第一個，並且依著裡面的指示行事。」聽完法師的話，他心裡由衷地感謝，帶著錦囊就回家了。

After listening to Michael, the monk asked to be excused[6] for a few minutes. And then came back with a few envelopes[7] in his hand, he said to Michael, "I have four envelopes for you. And each one of them is numbered[8]. Here's what you need to do. Tomorrow morning, please open envelope number one and follow the instructions[9] inside. After that, you may open the rest whenever you wish to."

Michael thanked the monk for his time. Feeling better, he went home with the four envelopes.

The next day, he woke up early. Remembering the instructions given to him by the monk. He opened the first envelope. The message within said, "Go for a walk in the mountains."

Surprised and puzzled[10], he thought, "Why should I go to the mountains for a walk? But since I agreed to follow the

第二天一早醒來，他依言打開第一個錦囊，上面寫著「到山上或者公園裡散步」。他頗為納悶，心想：為什麼要我到山上、公園散步呢？不過，既然法師這樣指示，那就不妨上山去吧！

到了山上，空氣清新，鳥語花香，眺望遠處的景色，真是美不勝收。突然間，他有感而發：「唉！這些年來只顧著賺錢，成天在工廠裡勤奮工作，竟不知還有這麼美好的一片天地？」當他欣賞著周遭美麗的景致之際，心情也頓時跟著喜悅起來了。

instructions, why not?"

Michael got ready and headed to the mountains.

When he arrived, he was greeted with fresh air, birds singing, and fragrant[11] flowers. Immediately, he felt a sense of calm and peace within himself.

He began to walk slowly, enjoying the scenery[12], thinking to himself, "Why have I worked so hard all these years? Working in my company day in and day out. I did not even know what I was missing. I should come here more often and be with nature!"

He spent the rest of the day in the mountains, and before heading home, he decided to open the second envelope. It said, "Greet your wife with a smile, speak good words, and praise[13] her."

Michael wondered[14] about the meaning behind this, but he was still willing to do as instructed[15].

Once he was home, he greeted his wife

接著他想起還有其他的錦囊，打開一看，第二個錦囊上面寫著「對太太微笑、說好、讚美」。這是什麼意思呢？雖然百思不解，也只有照做。一回到家，他便笑容可掬地對太太說：「太太，您辛苦了！今天打扮得好漂亮啊！」聽到先生如此讚美，太太當然十分歡喜，立刻準備了一桌佳肴回報。先生的心情也就更加愉悅了。

with a big smile, and said to her, "Thank you for working so hard every day. And you look beautiful today!"

His wife, though feeling awkward[16] as Michael rarely[17] gave her any praise, felt very happy and warm with his words. That evening she prepared a feast for him. Michael's mood was cheered even further.

The next day, Michael woke up, still feeling good about what happened the day before. He got ready for work, and before leaving the house, he opened the third envelope. It said, "Praise your staff."

When he arrived at his company, he greeted every person he met with, "Hello, thank you so much for being here." With Michael's fond[18] greetings, the whole company came alive with everyone feeling acknowledged[19] and they all worked even more efficiently[20].

After work, he decided to open the fourth

VOCABULARY

16. awkward (adj.) 尷尬的

17. rarely (adv.) 很少

18. fond (adj.) 溫柔的

19. acknowledged (adj.) 受認可的

20. efficiently (adv.) 高效地

隔天，他滿懷著歡喜心準備到工廠上班，再打開第三個錦囊。根據上面的指示「讚美部下」，他一到工廠，見人就說好：「科長好、組長好……」整個工廠的氣氛在他的帶動下，變得生氣蓬勃，大家都更加賣力地工作。

下班前，他打開第四個錦囊。依照上面的指示，他來到了海邊的沙灘上，並且在沙灘上寫下「煩惱」兩個字。「煩惱」才剛寫好，黃昏的潮水就湧上來，把字給沖掉了。這下子他才恍然大悟，原來去去來來，來來去去，一物不滯，才是真正的人生。

envelope. As instructed by the final envelope, he arrived at the beach and wrote the word "Worries" on the sand. As he finished writing the word, the high tide brought waves onto the shore and erased[21] his word on the sand.

At that moment, he suddenly realized[22], "Many things come and go. Coming and going is truly part of life."

As a Chan poem states, "In the presence[23] of plum blossoms, the same moon outside the window is thus different."

Everyone wishes for a happy life, but where is happiness? Happiness comes from ourselves, we are responsible[24] for creating our happiness. If we are willing to open up our hearts, embrace[25] others and accept the world, peace and happiness are everywhere.

VOCABULARY

21. erased (v.) 清除；擦掉；抹去
22. realized (v.) 明白；認識到；意識到
23. presence (n.) 存在；出現
24. responsible (adj.) 有責任的；應負責的
25. embrace (v.) 擁抱；包含

禪門有一首詩偈說：「平常一樣窗前月，才有梅花便不同。」大家都希望擁有快樂的人生，但快樂從哪裡來呢？快樂是自己創造出來的，只要我們願意敞開心胸，包容他人，接納世界，到處都有歡喜快樂。

Dharma Words by Venerable Master Hsing Yun

Be the one to start doing good deeds,
Be the one to start speaking good words,
Be the one to start thinking good thoughts.

星雲大師法語

好事從我做起，好話從我說起，好心從我生起。

notes

05

On Generosity

The Wooden Bowl

木 碗 的 故 事

Bodhi Light Tales
20-The Wooden Bowl

Once upon a time, there lived an old man who was confined[1] to bed by sickness. His youngest son, Andrew, took daily care of him. He would deliver his meals to his bedside every day.

Being old and fragile[2], the old man's hands would always shake uncontrollably. At mealtimes, his bowl would often slip from his hands. Thus, breaking his bowl had become the daily ritual[3] of mealtimes. Eventually, Andrew became most impatient and angry with his father for always breaking bowls whenever he ate.

Every time, he would complain to his father, "You always break your bowl! Can you please be more careful?! I don't make money for you to break bowls."

Feeling immensely[4] frustrated[5], Andrew thought, "I can't let this keep happening. I must do something about this." Being a carpenter,

有位老太太臥病在床，兒子每天都得送飯到房間裡給她吃。但是老太太因病手抖，飯碗經常不小心就從手中滑落地面而打破。兒子看了心裡很不高興，每次都向老太太抱怨：「妳常常把碗打破，我哪有這麼多錢買碗給妳用呢？」為此，兒子就去找來了一個木頭做成的碗，每天都以這個木碗盛飯給母親吃，這麼一來，即使飯碗不小心摔到地上，也不怕打破了。

Andrew was very good at woodwork[6]. And so, he came up with the idea of making a wooden bowl for his father.

"With this wooden bowl, it will never break even if Father drops it! No doubt[7], it will save me time and money," Andrew said proudly to himself.

From then on, he began to serve his father's meals using only the wooden bowl. At first, everything seemed to work out so well.

One day, Andrew found his son playing in the garden. His son's attention[8] was very focused on a wooden block as he was chipping[9] away, trying his very best to carve[10] out the wood.

Curious, Andrew asked his son, "What are you doing, my son? What are you carving?"

"I'm trying to make a wooden bowl," his son replied.

VOCABULARY

6. woodwork (n.) 木製品
7. no doubt (phrase) 毫無疑問；無庸置疑
8. attention (n.) 注意力
9. chipping (v.) 削
10. carve (v.) 雕刻

有一天，老太太的孫子在院子裡玩耍，弄了個木頭在那裡刻刻挖挖的。父親看了感到好奇，就問：「兒子啊！你拿個木頭在那裡刻刻挖挖的，幹什麼呢？」

「我在刻碗，刻一個木頭的碗。」

「你刻木頭的碗做什麼用？」

「等你老了，我拿木碗盛飯給你吃，你就不會把碗打破了呀！」

Taken aback, Andrew asked, "A wooden bowl? Why do you need a wooden bowl?"

"The bowl is for you, Father. When you grow old, I will serve your meals only with this wooden bowl. And so, like Grandpa, you will not break it!"

Feeling much surprised[11] and ashamed[12], Andrew realized that whatever he did, his son would seek to follow. He realized he was setting an example for his son. If he treated[13] his own father as he did, then his son would certainly treat him in the same way in the future.

This story highlights the following scenario[14]. In any hospital, the children's ward is often busy with parents visiting their children. This is in contrast[15] to the ward for the elderly, which is much quieter with very few visitors. The children of elderly people do not visit them as much or bring them food when they

VOCABULARY

11. surprised (adj.) 感到驚訝的
12. ashamed (adj.) 羞愧的；慚愧的
13. treated (v.) 對待
14. scenario (n.) 情節；情景
15. contrast (n.) 對比；差別

父親給兒子這麼一說，慚愧得無地自容，方才警覺到今日自己怎麼對待老母親，將來兒子就會怎麼對待自己；兒子對自己的行為可是看得一清二楚呀！

do visit. However, when their children do come, they would surely bring a voice recorder. Upon the last breath, their children would often demand of them their share of the inheritance[16] due from their parents. Sadly, the voice recorder is only used as proof of such inheritance.

In today's society, the following question has become a growing concern[17]: why have we become so cold?

There is a poem that describes this distress[18], "I can still recall the time when I raised my son, and now my own son is raising my grandson. I can accept it if my own son lets me suffer in hunger. However, I do not wish for my grandson to treat my son that way."

This poem expresses the unconditional[19] love that parents have towards their own children. Parents are ready to work tirelessly for their children, and are willing to take on any burden[20] and suffering so that their children are in comfort and at ease.

It is a great wish for every child to always remember

VOCABULARY

16. inheritance (n.) 遺產
17. concern (n.) 關心；掛念
18. distress (n.) 苦惱
19. unconditional (adj.) 無條件的
20. burden (n.) 負擔

我曾經在同一家醫院裡看到這樣的情形，兒童的病房總是有好多父母進進出出照顧孩子，老人的病房卻很少有兒女前去探望，縱使有，也不全都是帶水果、帶奶粉去探望，而是帶錄音機。兒女一來到父母的病榻前，就將錄音機朝床頭一放，說：「爸爸媽媽你說吧，你的遺產將來要交給誰？」現在的社會竟然走到這種地步，實在令人堪憂。

that it is a blessing to have their parents around. Take the time to recall[21] all the good times as a family we had as children. What were the lessons our parents taught us, what did we learn from them?

As children, we should acknowledge[22] that our parents did whatever they could with whatever they had. We can express[23] our endless[24] gratitude[25] to our parents by talking with them, spending time with them, and letting them know that we care and love them as much as they cared and loved us.

VOCABULARY

21. recall (v.) 回想；回憶
22. acknowledge (v.) 感激；答謝
23. express (v.) 表達；表露；陳述
24. endless (adj.) 無窮盡的；無盡的
25. gratitude (n.) 感恩

有首詩偈說：「記得當初我養兒，我兒今又養孫兒，我兒餓我由他餓，莫教孫兒餓我兒。」可謂道盡了天下父母心，寧可自己受累，也要兒女溫飽。但願天下兒女都能喚回對父母的孝心，明白有父母在堂是莫大的福氣！

Dharma Words by Venerable Master Hsing Yun

Anger and hatred are the roots of troubles.
Gratitude and contentment are the sources of happiness.

星雲大師法語

瞋怒怨恨，是煩惱的根本。
感恩知足，是快樂的泉源。

notes

06

On Generosity

Life-Saving

救媳婦

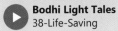

Scan me to listen!

掃我，聆聽故事！

Once upon a time in Taipei, there lived a surgeon[1] named Martin. He had received an invitation to a medical conference[2] in London. So, he booked his ticket but, due to the peak season[3], had to transit via Hong Kong International Airport. As a frequent flyer[4] and a gold status member, the airline had reserved his preferred seat for him.

On the day of his flight, Martin had made arrangements[5] with his friend to have a quick catch-up before his flight. However, his friend waited for over an hour at Taipei International Airport, yet Martin was nowhere to be found. As time inched closer to boarding time, Martin's friend became anxious and thought it unusual for Martin to not show up without a phone call. He tried calling Martin several times but there was no answer.

What had happened was, on the way to the airport, Martin was caught in a traffic jam due to a terrible accident. As Martin's car passed the scene of the accident, he saw that the driver, a

VOCABULARY

1. surgeon (n.) 外科醫生
2. medical conference (n.) 醫學會議
3. peak season (n.) 旺季
4. frequent flyer (n.) 飛行常客
5. arrangements (n.) 安排

台北有一位醫生,受邀請到英國倫敦參加一個醫學會議,他買好了機票,要先到香港轉機,航空公司都給他排好了機位,結果時間到了卻沒有去搭飛機,在桃園機場等著送行的朋友覺得奇怪,打電話也查不到人,為什麼呢?

lady, was bleeding severely. Martin then asked the taxi driver to stop the car. He exited the vehicle, and informed the police officers, "I'm a doctor, please let me help."

At that moment, catching his flight was no longer important to him. All he could think of was how to save the young lady's life. He quickly grabbed[6] a clean cloth and did what he could to stop the bleeding. Soon, the ambulance arrived. However, as her condition was quite unstable[7], Martin felt he couldn't just leave his patient in her current state, and so decided to accompany[8] her in the ambulance to the hospital and handle the surgery himself.

Once the surgical operation[9] was finished, Martin quickly called his friend to apologize[10] and explained what happened. Afterward, he booked himself on the next available flight. By the time he arrived in London, the conference was already halfway over. Since Martin's sole purpose for being in London was the medical conference, he flew back to Taiwan as soon as it ended.

Martin's son, Alan, came to pick him up at

VOCABULARY

6. grabbed (v.) 抓取
7. unstable (adj.) 不穩定的
8. accompany (v.) 陪同
9. surgical operation (n.) 外科手術；手術
10. apologize (v.) 道歉

原來他在去機場的路上遇到一起車禍，一位少女受傷流血，情況危急，他善心一動，也顧不得趕飛機了，立刻下車對那位少女施救，又親自把少女送到醫院做縫合手術，這一耽擱，飛機當然趕不上了，只好重新安排，等他抵達倫敦的時候，那個醫學會議已經進行了一半。

the airport and brought along a friend.

After hugging his father, Alan said to him, "Dad, I would like you to meet Priscilla, thank you for saving her life."

Martin looked puzzled and confused[11], so Alan explained, "She is the young lady you saved on your way to the airport."

"Oh! Is that right? It is a pleasure to meet you, I hope you are recovering well. How do you two know each other then?" Martin asked.

Alan continued, "We have been dating for over a year now. Sorry, I never introduced her to you. It is because Priscilla's father does not approve[12] of our relationship. He cannot accept his daughter marrying the son of a doctor, because not long ago, Priscilla's mother fell ill and was treated by an experienced doctor. However, despite the doctor's best efforts, her mother died. Priscilla's father is still overwhelmed[13] with grief whenever he hears about doctors. However, on the day of Priscilla's accident, it was a matter of life and death, and a doctor saved her life. Your decision to save her had prevented[14] her from becoming paralyzed[15]."

VOCABULARY

11. confused (adj.) 困惑的
12. approve (v.) 贊成；稱許
13. overwhelmed (v.) 充斥著；受打擊
14. prevented (v.) 防止；避免
15. paralyzed (adj.) 癱瘓的

開完會，他垂頭喪氣地回到台灣，他兒子卻帶著那個少女在機場接他，跟他說：「爸爸，謝謝您挽救了我們的婚姻。」

原來那個少女就是他兒子的女朋友，他兒子追求了一年多，女方父親一直不同意，說什麼都不准女兒嫁給醫生的兒子，因為女兒的媽媽是被一個庸醫醫死的，所以恨透了醫生。

"I just did what any doctor would do." Martin replied and then turned to Priscilla, "I'm sorry to hear about your loss. How is your father?"

"My father is very glad that he still has me. That's why I want to thank you. Because of you, my father has overcome his grief and mindset[16] about doctors. He realized that not all doctors are bad. My mother may have lost her life due to a doctor, but it was a doctor who saved mine. My father has even given his blessing to us. I can never thank you enough!! If you had not stopped to help, I perhaps would not even be here today," Priscilla said with tears streaming down her cheeks.

Extremely touched, Martin hugged Priscilla and said, "All I could think about was to save a life, who would have thought that the person would be my future daughter-in-law? It was just meant to be."

This story highlights that in life, we are bound to encounter[17] heartaches and misfortunes[18]. But if we lose hope, feel trapped[19] in misery[20], or turn selfish,

想不到女兒出了車禍，生死一瞬間，卻又被醫生救活過來，僥倖沒有成為殘廢，而這個醫生恩人，偏偏又是女兒男友的父親，這一來，他就不好意思再反對下去，終於成全了這一對小兒女的婚姻。這位醫生知道這一番前因後果以後，不禁驚嘆：「我當初只想到要把那個受傷的少女救活，沒想到反而救了自己的媳婦，真是老天有眼！」

we blind ourselves to good causes and conditions. As a result, we miss out on good outcomes unhoped for. Consider Martin's act of goodness, though he helped Priscilla out of his resolve[21] as a doctor, he helped his own son and future daughter-in-law. Furthermore, Priscilla's father was able to change his perception[22] of doctors due to the kindness shown to his daughter.

If we have a compassionate heart and a mind free from discrimination[23], we can spread compassion throughout the world. We will act selflessly[24] to help those in need, and the ensuing[25] good causes and conditions will bring favorable results.

VOCABULARY

21. resolve (n.) 決定之事；決心
22. perception (n.) 感覺
23. discrimination (n.) 岐視
24. selflessly (adv.) 無私地
25. ensuing (adj.) 隨後的

人倘若心懷成見，就將錯失一段良緣。世間的因緣很美妙，時時心懷慈悲，熱心助人，把溫馨飄香人間，美好的因緣也能開花結果。

Dharma Words by Venerable Master Hsing Yun

To bear good or bad fruit depends on good or bad causes and conditions;
Every person is their own gardener.
The result of our actions, good or bad, depends on our good or ill will;
As we are the master of our own will.
Our mind is like a field that produces when fertilized.
Generosity is like seeds sown that yield a good harvest.

星雲大師法語

種善因得善果，種惡因得惡果，人是自己的園丁。

存好心得好報，存歹心得歹報，心是自己的主人。

心地如田地，田地肥沃，才能種植。

布施如播種，播種善緣，才能收成。

notes

07

On Generosity

One-Legged Duck

鴨子一條腿

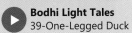

Bodhi Light Tales
39-One-Legged Duck

Once upon a time, there was a CEO named Richard. Under his skilled management, his business grew steadily. Richard was a serious and stern[1] man. At work, everyone knew of his high expectations and his sharp eye for details.

At home, Richard likewise showed no affection[2] toward his wife, nor did he ever praise her. They had been married for more than ten years with no children. Every day, Jane would carefully prepare delicious food for Richard. She would always make him three-course meals, hoping to impress[3] him. However, Richard never appreciated[4] or praised her efforts. Instead, he simply ate the food in silence and then left to concern[5] himself with work or other things.

One day, Richard was home for lunch. Jane had cooked a steamed duck especially for him. When they were both seated, Richard reached

VOCABULARY

1. stern (adj.) 嚴肅的
2. affection (n.) 感情;愛情
3. impress (v.) 留下深刻印象
4. appreciated (v.) 欣賞;感激
5. concern (v.) 關心

王先生是一家公司的董事長,生意做得非常成功,但是個性嚴肅,太太每天用心做飯菜,從來都不曾獲得先生的一句讚美。

有一天,王先生回家吃中飯,太太特地為他做了一道清蒸板鴨。可是正當王先生舉起筷子要享用美味的時候,卻發現鴨子有異狀。於是他問:「太太!鴨子一般都是兩條腿,為什麼我們家的鴨子只有一條腿呢?」

太太回答:「沒錯啊!我們家裡的鴨子都只有一條腿啊!」

for the food but, as he was about to pick up the drumstick[6], he realized something strange, so he turned to his wife, "Don't ducks usually have two legs? Why is there only one drumstick on this plate?"

"Oh...Didn't you know that all the ducks raised in this house only have one leg?" Jane replied.

Dumbfounded[7], Richard said, "Utter[8] nonsense[9]! Ducks ALWAYS have two legs, how can they have only one?"

"If you don't believe me, we can go to the backyard and take a look," said Jane.

Richard immediately[10] put down his chopsticks and got up, "Sure! Let's go now."

"All right!" Jane said.

Making their way to the backyard, Jane quietly opened the gate, as the ducks were sleeping.

As expected, all of them stood on one leg,

VOCABULARY

6. drumstick (n.) 雞腿
7. dumbfounded (adj.) 目瞪口呆的
8. utter (adj.) 絕對；完全
9. nonsense (n.) 胡說；胡扯
10. immediately (adv.) 立刻；立即

先生不相信，說：「亂講！鴨子都是兩條腿，怎麼會是一條腿呢？」

太太說：「如果你不相信，就到我們家後院的池塘去看看吧！」

日正當中，兩人來到了後院。果不其然，三五成群的鴨子都在休息，全都蜷起了一條腿。這時，太太就說了：「你看！我們家的鴨子不都是一條腿嗎？」

so Jane said proudly, "See! I told you that our ducks only have one leg!"

Richard smiled, but also had a trick up his sleeve[11]. He slowly raised his hands and then started clapping, "Clap! Clap! Clap!" All the ducks woke up in shock, and immediately ran around like crazy, not knowing what had just happened.

Richard turned to his wife and said smugly[12], "Do you see? Our ducks DO have two legs, not one!"

Jane was prepared to use this opportunity to say what she had long held back, "Can't YOU see that only by applauding[13] will these ducks have two legs!!"

This story highlights that giving others praise is very important. Who in this world does not like to be praised and acknowledged[14] by others? For a family to be happy and harmonious[15], it requires every member of the family to come together to make it so.

VOCABULARY

11. had a trick up his sleeve (phrase) 暗中留有一招；使出招數

12. smugly (adv.) 自鳴得意地

13. applauding (v.) 稱讚；讚賞

14. acknowledged (v.) 公認；承認

15. harmonious (adj.) 和睦的；和諧的

先生倒也很高明，立刻對著鴨群拍起手來，「啪！啪！啪！」掌聲一起，鴨子受到了驚嚇，紛紛跑了起來。先生甚為得意，就說：「太太，妳看吧！我們家的鴨子不也是兩條腿嗎？」

王太太見時機成熟，就對先生說：「難道你不知道嗎？這是有掌聲才有兩條腿的啊！」

For a loving couple, as in this story, a husband must praise his wife, letting her know that she is the most beautiful and kind woman in the world. A wife must, in turn, let her husband know that he is the most capable[16] and willing man in the world.

Without a doubt, if we respond to each other in kind ways with praise and acknowledgments, the relationship may last for a lifetime. Often when we interact[17] with others, we like to cut to the chase[18].

However, if we speak kindly and with encouragement[19], such words become powerful, surpassing[20] any physical strength.

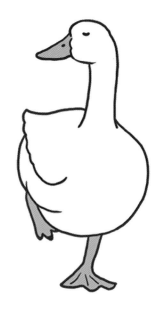

一個幸福安樂的家庭，需要仰賴家中的每一份子共同來營造，上下相親相愛。尤其做先生的，要讚美太太是世間上最賢慧、最美好的女人；做妻子的，也要讚美先生是最能幹、最有為的男人，夫妻相互讚美，必然就能白頭偕老。

讚美對於人是非常重要的，舉世滔滔哪一個人不希望獲得別人的讚美、肯定？所以，做人處事要想得到方便，有時候口中的一句好話，比出多少的力氣助人，力量還要來得更大。

Dharma Words by Venerable Master Hsing Yun

Better a smile than a fragrant flower.
Better a thought than clear water.
Better a poem than a symphony.
Better a praise than poetry.

星雲大師法語

一束鮮花，不如一臉微笑。
一杯清水，不如一念清明。
一曲音樂，不如一句好話。
一首詩歌，不如一聲讚歎。

08

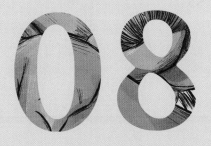

On Generosity

The Royal Beggar

乞女變皇后

Bodhi Light Tales
41-The Royal Beggar

Scan me to listen!

掃我，聆聽故事！

Once upon a time, there lived a lady named Mila, who was homeless and begged[1] for a living. One day, Mila went begging for food. As she walked past a temple, a Dharma service[2] was going on, and she saw many people making all kinds of offerings. Some of them offered candles or incense, others offered flowers, fruits, or even food.

Feeling inspired, Mila thought, "I wish I too could make an offering, but I have nothing to offer."

As she thought about making an offering and feeling disappointed[3], she put her hand in her pocket, and to her surprise, she found something.

"What's this? How come I have a penny[4] in my pocket?" Then she remembered that last week, someone gave her a penny and she had forgotten about it. So, happily, she followed everyone into the temple to make her offering.

As she entered the temple, she heard the Buddhist hymns[5] and felt calm and peaceful.

VOCABULARY

1. begged (v.) 乞討
2. Dharma service (n.) 法會
3. disappointed (adj.) 失望的
4. penny (n.) 一分錢
5. Buddhist hymns (n.) 梵唄

有一位以乞討維生的貧窮女孩，一天經過一座寺廟，適逢法會期間，她看到很多人在打齋、點燈、做種種布施，心裡很羨慕，就想：我一個靠乞討過日子的女孩，沒有什麼錢，怎麼布施呢？她一面想，一面摸摸口袋，咦！不曉得什麼時候撿到了一個銅錢？隨即，她高興地拿著這個銅錢，跟著大家就去布施、結緣了。

As she enjoyed the sounds of the Dharma instruments[6] and chanting, a monk approached[7] her and said, "Welcome, would you like to offer incense?"

"Um...can I?" Feeling slightly embarrassed[8], Mila took the incense stick and said, "Thank you."

Mila walked in front of the Buddha, knelt and prayed. When she was finished, she took out her penny and dropped it into the donation box. As Mila was leaving the shrine, a monk stopped her and said, "Excuse me, could you please wait? Our Abbot would like to meet you."

Soon the Abbot appeared and greeted Mila, "Auspicious blessings[9] to you."

Mila stood with her palms joined, feeling anxious[10] and not knowing what to say.

The Abbot said, "I heard you made an offering today, I wanted to come and thank you personally. Please follow me."

Mila followed the Abbot to the center of

乞女布施的消息傳出去之後，住持大和尚被她的真心感動，便親自來為她誦經祝福。

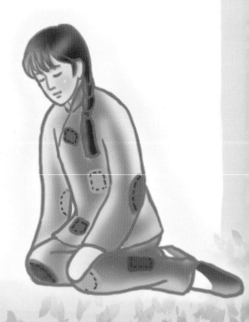

the shrine. The Abbot laid three prostrations[11] to the Buddha and began chanting. In the end, a prayer was dedicated[12] to Mila and her family.

Equally touched and baffled[13], Mila said to the Abbot, "Thank you so much. You didn't have to do all that for me, I am just a beggar with nothing."

The Abbot replied, "You gave everything you had, I see before me a sincere person with a good heart."

Mila left the temple feeling grateful and fulfilled. From that day on, though she continued to be a beggar, she felt different, more at peace with herself.

A few months later, the whole nation was in mourning[14]. The queen had passed away and the King was inconsolable[15]. The royal ministers saw how unhappy the King was, so they suggested an outing, and the King agreed.

That afternoon, they arrived at a forest,

VOCABULARY

11. prostrations (n.) 禮拜
12. dedicated (v.) 獻給
13. baffled (adj.) 被迷惑的
14. mourning (n.) 哀痛；哀悼
15. inconsolable (adj.)
    無法安慰的；極為傷心的

過不多久，這個國家的皇后去世，國王非常悲傷。大臣們見國王成天悶悶不樂，都鼓勵他出外打獵遊玩散心。當國王來到了山林，遠遠就看到前方的樹下大放光明，走近一看，發現光芒竟然是來自一位乞丐女孩的身上。這位女孩雖然衣衫襤褸，卻長得眉清目秀，國王一歡喜，就把她帶回了宮中，讓她沐浴盥洗，換上新裝。

and from afar saw a beam[16] of light shining on a tree. As they got closer, they realized that the light shone on a lady sitting under the tree. The lady was Mila, sitting in meditation. Despite[17] her ragged[18] appearance, beauty flowed from her. The ministers told the King about Mila, and feeling sorry for her, the King decided to bring her back with him to the palace.

Back at the palace, Mila was given new clothes and lodgings[19]. Feeling grateful, Mila would spend her time comforting the King with stories. As the months passed, the King fell in love with Mila and decided to marry her and crown her queen.

After becoming the queen, Mila reflected[20] on her life's journey and thought that she must have done something good in her past. Suddenly, she remembered the temple and the offering she had made.

The next day, she proposed to the king that

VOCABULARY

16. beam (n.) 光線；光束
17. despite (prep.) 儘管
18. ragged (adj.) 衣衫襤褸的
19. lodgings (n.) 寄宿的地方
20. reflected (v.) 深思；認真思考

經過裝扮的女孩，就像仙女般美麗，漸漸地，國王就喜歡上她，立她做了皇后。

從乞討的貧女，搖身一變成為皇后之尊，她想一定是布施的功德，才有這樣的福德因緣，便準備了十大車的金錢寶物，載送到寺廟裡打齋供僧。

she would go make an offering[21] to the temple. The King agreed and asked his ministers to prepare ten wagons[22] filled with offerings.

So, the queen traveled to the temple followed by the ten wagons of offerings. When she arrived, Mila was greeted by a monk. She nodded[23] to him and went straight to the shrine[24]. She waited only for a few minutes, but soon became irritated[25] and said to the monk, "Where is the Abbot? In the past, when I came to offer a penny, the Abbot personally came to thank me. He even chanted and prayed for me and my family. Now I am the queen and come with enough offerings to fill ten wagons. The Abbot should have greeted me upon my arrival, but instead, I am greeted by a simple monk."

VOCABULARY

21. offering (n.) 供養；供品
22. wagons (n.) 四輪馬車
23. nodded (v.) 點頭致意；點頭示意
24. shrine (n.) 殿堂
25. irritated (adj.) 惱火的；生氣的

可是這一天供齋的時候，只有知客師出來迎接。她很納悶，就問：「以前只有一枚銅錢的布施，住持和尚就親自為我誦經、祝福，為什麼現今我成為皇后了，用幾千萬倍的財物來布施，反而只是知客師父出來招待呢？」

The humble[26] monk said, "I am very sorry, Your Majesty, our Abbot wanted me to deliver a message to you. In the past, you were a beggar, a penny was all you had. When you made that offering long ago, it was from your heart and utterly[27] sincere. That kind of offering is worth more than anything. But today, though you come with ten wagons of offerings, you have also brought along your arrogance[28]. In truth, this kind of offering means very little. There is no need for our Abbot to meet with you. A humble monk like me is more than good enough for the likes of you."

This story highlights that the merit born from an act of generosity does not lie in the quantity given, instead it arises from our mindset[29] and attitude when giving.

Are we truly sincere and selfless[30] in the moment of giving?

Or are we selfish and self-centered, thinking only

VOCABULARY

26. humble (adj.) 謙遜的

27. utterly (adv.) 完全；絕對

28. arrogance (n.) 傲慢態度；自大

29. mindset (n.) 心態

30. selfless (adj.) 無私心的；無私欲的

知客師就告訴她：「當初妳是個貧窮的乞丐，布施的銅錢雖然微少，卻是你傾盡所有，那種虔敬布施的心意是比天地都還要大的。現在，妳帶著高傲、我慢的心而來，雖然看上去是十大車的金錢供養，實際上卻是很微薄的，就不需要大和尚來為妳誦經祝福，只要知客師接待就夠了。」

about the reward or what we gain in return?

Just like Mila, when only a beggar she offered the only thing she had with utmost sincerity and respect. After becoming queen, she sought to offer with a discriminative[31] and egotistical[32] mind. It is important to remember that when we give, it must always be with our utmost sincerity and respect. This kind of selfless giving will always surpass[33] all other forms of giving.

There is a saying, "A fragrant[34] mind can spread in all directions." This means that our mindset and attitude determine the results of our actions.

VOCABULARY

31. discriminative (adj.) 有分別心的
32. egotistical (adj.) 自我本位的；任性的
33. surpass (v.) 勝過
34. fragrant (adj.) 芳香的；芬芳的

　　從這一件事情我們可以知道，功德的大小不光是從金錢的多少來計算，主要還是看你的心意虔不虔誠。所謂「心香一瓣，普遍十方」，有時候，你能以一顆恭敬、誠懇的心做好事，甚至比金錢的布施還要來得重要。

Dharma Words by Venerable Master Hsing Yun

Contented people are rich.
Greedy people are poor.
Those who help are noble.
Those who desire much are degraded.

星雲大師法語

知足者富，貪心者貧，
助人者貴，多欲者賤。

notes

09

On Generosity

A Bowl of Noodles

一 碗 麵

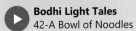

Bodhi Light Tales
42-A Bowl of Noodles

Once upon a time, there was a high school student named Annie, who lived with her mother. One thing she feared[1] most coming home from school was her mother's non-stop gossiping[2] and complaining.

One day, Annie came home after a bad day at school. She opened the door, and there her mother was, in the living room, waiting for her.

Annie just wanted to go straight into her room, but her mother called out, "Aren't you going to say hello? How was school today?"

Before Annie could answer, her mother said, "I just got off the phone with Mrs. Cooper, she told me her daughter cooked dinner last night. And her son is helping with the gardening and planning their family trip…"

Annie rolled[3] her eyes and slowly edged[4] towards her bedroom. However, her mother continued, "Are you listening to me? You should be helping me with the household chores[5] too; you never cook, you never do anything for me…"

Upon hearing this, Annie couldn't hold

VOCABULARY

1. feared (v.) 害怕；感到顧慮
2. gossiping (n.) 閒言閒語
3. rolled (v.) 翻滾
4. edged (v.) 徐徐移動
5. chores (n.) 日常瑣事；雜務

有一位女學生，因為母親經常對她嘮叨不停，讓她覺得很反感。有一天，當母親又叨叨絮絮說個沒完的時候，她終於忍耐不住，脫口說：「妳別再嘮叨了！」氣呼呼的她，話一說完，便奪門而出，離家出走。

herself back anymore, she cut in and shouted in frustration[6], "I've had enough! Your gossiping and complaining must stop! I won't take this anymore! I'm leaving!"

Annie stormed out[7] of the house, determined[8] to get as far away as possible.

Having spent hours walking around town, Annie was tired and it was already late. She sat down at a bus stop and then realized that her stomach was rumbling[9]. She could smell food nearby and as she looked around, she saw a noodle shop just around the corner. Annie quickly got up and walked over. She looked at the menu, and just as she was about to order a bowl of noodles, she reached into her pocket. With great disappointment[10], Annie realized she forgot to bring her purse.

The shop owner welcomed Annie and asked, "Young lady, what would you like?"

Annie shook her head and looked down.

VOCABULARY

6. frustration (n.) 無奈
7. stormed out (v.) 衝出去
8. determined (adj.) 下定決心的；堅決的
9. rumbling (v.) 發出咕嚕咕嚕的聲音
10. disappointment (n.) 失望

傍晚時分，徘徊路上多時的女學生，肚子已經餓得嘰哩咕嚕叫，正巧經過路邊一處麵攤，便決定就近叫碗麵來吃。但是，站在麵攤前，她掏掏口袋，才發現自己出門時竟連一毛錢都沒有帶。這下怎麼辦呢？

老板見她面有難色的樣子，熱情地上前招呼她：「小姑娘，妳要吃麵嗎？」女學生結結巴巴地說：「我是想吃麵……可是……身上沒有帶錢。」好心的老板立刻就說：「沒關係，我請妳吃吧！」隨即就煮了一碗麵給她止飢。

She thought to herself, "Why did I forget to bring money? What am I going to do? I am so hungry. I am not even sure if I have the energy to get home?"

The owner politely asked again, "Would you like some noodles?"

Highly embarrassed[11], Annie answered, "Yes, I would love some noodles, but I left my money at home."

The owner saw how worried[12] Annie looked and said, "Well, you know what? You're in luck! You are my last customer today, so your noodles will be on the house[13]!"

He then began to cook the noodles, adding extra vegetables and broth[14] to the bowl. When the noodles were served, Annie was so hungry she couldn't wait to eat. As she ate a few mouthfuls, tears began trickling[15] down her cheeks.

The owner, who kept watching her,

VOCABULARY

11. embarrassed (adj.) 不好意思；尷尬的
12. worried (adj.) 憂慮的；發愁的
13. on the house (phrase) 由商家免費提供的
14. broth (n.) 肉湯
15. trickling (v.) 滴流

asked, "You don't like the noodles?"

Annie quickly wiped[16] her tears and replied, "No, not at all…I just thought of my mother, she never had anything good to say to me, she always complains and compares[17] me with other people. Mostly, she either criticizes[18] me for something I didn't do or blames[19] me for what I did. I am never good enough for her! You, on the other hand, are so kind to me, and you don't even know me. I feel really touched[20], thank you so much!"

On hearing what Annie just said, the owner shook his head and replied, "Well… I've only given you a bowl of noodles, yet you feel so touched. But, have you ever put yourself in your mother's shoes? How many meals has

VOCABULARY

16. wiped (v.) 擦
17. compares (v.) 比較
18. criticizes (v.) 批評；批判；指責
19. blames (v.) 責備；責怪
20. touched (adj.) 感激的；令人感動的

當女學生接下這碗熱騰騰的麵，吃著吃著突然就流下了淚水。老板一看，便問：「小姑娘，不好吃嗎？」

女學生趕緊說：「不是的。我是想到母親天天罵我、怪我，而妳與我素昧平生，卻對我這麼好，我內心真是百感交集啊！」

老板聽他這麼一講，搖搖頭說：「唉！我才給妳一碗麵吃，就讓妳這麼感動，可是妳回想一下，妳的母親煮了多少頓飯菜給妳吃呀！」

she cooked for you? I'm sure that despite her complaints, she means well."

Shocked by his words, Annie realized she had been thoughtless[21] and selfish. She felt bad for snapping[22] at her mother without understanding her true intentions[23]. After finishing the noodles, she thanked the owner and quickly made her way home.

As she neared home, she saw her mother had been waiting for her by the door. Looking anxious[24], she asked Annie, "Where have you been? I was worried sick! Anyway, the food is cold now, I'll heat it for you! So come in and have dinner!"

This story highlights[25] the hearts of all parents. Many parents wish to express their love and care towards their children in the best possible ways. Some express through giving advice like: Do well at school and make us proud, or do more exercise and look after yourself, or don't go out partying too much, or don't

VOCABULARY

21. thoughtless (adj.) 不為他人著想的；粗心的
22. snapping (v.) 厲聲說；謾罵
23. intentions (n.) 目的；意圖
24. anxious (adj.) 憂慮的；焦急的
25. highlights (v.) 強調

女學生一聽，恍然大悟，對於自己的任性無知，感到相當慚愧。吃完了麵，向老板道謝之後，趕緊跑回家。還沒到家，遠遠地，就看見母親站在門口張望。母親看到女兒回來，焦急地說：「唉呀！妳跑到哪裡去？飯菜都涼了，趕快進來吃！」

stay up late, sleep early and so on.

In this story, Annie's mother believes she is showing Annie how much she cares for her. However, Annie felt she was just complaining. This is an instance of mutual[26] misunderstanding. How can parents show their care without sounding inconsiderate[27]? How can children express their thoughts and feelings effectively[28]?

Truth be told, nobody can really get the best of both worlds[29].

As parents, caring for our children is no doubt a blessing. However, the needs and feelings of our children must be taken into account. It is vital[30] to give them time and space to find themselves. It is equally vital to let them know we are there for them when they need us.

As children, understanding the true intentions of our parents is just as important. We must put

VOCABULARY

26. mutual (adj.) 共同的；共有的
27. inconsiderate (adj.) 不體諒別人的；不為他人著想的
28. effectively (adv.) 有效地
29. the best of both worlds (phrase) 兩全其美
30. vital (adj.) 極其重要的

所謂「天下父母心」，許多父母出於對子女的關愛，總會不時給予叮嚀：你要用功讀書、你要注意身體健康……你不要到處玩樂、你不要熬夜……實在說，世間事難以兩全其美，雖然父母關懷兒女，有時候也應該考量兒女的需要與感受，而身為兒女的人，也不能不體諒父母的一片愛心，甚至應該反觀自省：我有對父母噓寒問暖嗎？家庭裡的成員要能夠互相關懷，彼此問候，才不枉成為一家人的好因好緣。

ourselves in their shoes[31] and ask ourselves often: What have we done for our parents lately? Have we shown them enough care? Even more so, this self-reflection[32] extends[33] to our family as a whole. What about the rest of our family? Have we shown them that we do care?

VOCABULARY

31. put ourselves in their shoes (phrase) 從他們的角度考慮
32. self-reflection (n.) 自我反省
33. extends (v.) 伸展；延伸

Dharma Words by Venerable Master Hsing Yun

As parents, we should be perfectly willing to raise our children.

As teachers, we should be perfectly willing to educate our students.

As students, we should be perfectly willing to listen and learn.

As sons and daughters, we should be perfectly willing to love and care for our parents.

星雲大師法語

為人父母，要心甘情願養育子女；

為人師長，要心甘情願作育英才；

為人學生，要心甘情願承受教誨；

為人子女，要心甘情願孝養父母。

notes

10

On Generosity

The Happy Mom Washing Machine

媽媽樂

Bodhi Light Tales
43-Happy Mom Washing Machine

Scan me to listen!
掃我，聆聽故事！

Once upon a time, there lived a widow[1] named Mary. After ten years of marriage, her husband passed away, leaving her and their two children, Bryan and Isabel, behind. Life was difficult for Mary as her husband did not leave her with much money. So, Mary took on cleaning jobs to make ends meet[2].

Every day, Mary had to clean for three families. On top of that, she provided laundry services[3] for people too. Often, she would work quite late into the night. Bryan and Isabel would often ask her, "Mom, when will you have time to take us to the park?" Mary would always answer them, "When I'm done with the laundry." Though Bryan and Isabel wished their mother could spend more time with them, they understood she was working hard to give them a good life. Otherwise, their schooling would cost too much, not to mention[4] providing daily necessities[5].

VOCABULARY

1. widow (n.) 寡婦
2. make ends meet (phrase) 勉強維持生計；使收支平衡
3. laundry services (n.) 洗衣服務
4. not to mention (phrase) 更不用說；更何況
5. daily necessities (n.) 日用品

有一位母親，由於先生早逝，獨立一人撫養幾個小兒女。因為家裡貧寒，沒有什麼收入，這名母親就以幫人家洗衣服維持家計。每天到各戶人家收回衣服洗，經常洗到三更半夜，實在很辛苦。幾個小兒女也體諒母親賺錢不容易，為了給他們吃飯，為了替他們交學費而這麼勞累。所以，他們也在平常節省一塊錢、五毛錢，存到撲滿裡。

One day, after school, Bryan asked Isabel, "What do you think we can do to help Mom?"

Isabel answered, "We could help her do the laundry!"

Bryan then said, "But Mom wouldn't let us help...I'm sure she would say go and do your homework or something like that..."

Isabel thought for a while and replied, "How about we save one dollar a day from our pocket money? After saving for a while, we can get a washing machine[6] for our mom!"

Bryan replied excitedly[7], "Yes! That's a great idea!"

And so, starting that day, every day, Bryan and Isabel would drop one dollar or any small change[8] they had into their piggy bank[9].

After a whole year, the piggy bank was filled with money. Bryan then decided to go to an appliance store[10] with the piggy bank.

VOCABULARY

6. washing machine (n.) 洗衣機
7. excitedly (adv.) 興奮地
8. small change (n.) 零錢
9. piggy bank (n.) 撲滿
10. appliance store (n.) 電器行

When he arrived at the store, he said to the owner, "I'd like to buy a washing machine please." Back in those days, a washing machine would cost only a little more than a thousand dollars.

The owner looked at Bryan, and seeing the piggy bank under his arm, said, "Okay, we have different models[11], is there one, in particular, you're looking for?"

Bryan said, "Um...I'm not sure. But this is all the money I have."

And then Bryan opened the piggy bank and began counting the money. Unfortunately[12], once he'd counted it all, Bryan realized[13] he was still thirty dollars short for even the cheapest model.

Feeling embarrassed[14] that he did not have enough money and feeling disappointed[15], Bryan said to the owner, "I'm sorry, I don't have enough money...I'll come back another time.

VOCABULARY

11.   models (n.) 模型；型號
12.   unfortunately (adv.) 不幸地；可惜的是
13.   realized (v.) 意識到
14.   embarrassed (adj.) 不好意思；尷尬的
15.   disappointed (adj.) 失望的；沮喪的

經過一、兩年，大兒子覺得撲滿裡的錢不少了，抱著撲滿拿到電器行，告訴老板要買一台洗衣機。在一、二十年前，要一千多塊錢才買得到一台洗衣機。小朋友把撲滿裡的錢拿出來數，最後還差了三十幾塊錢。

這小孩覺得很不好意思，本來以為錢夠了，想不到少了三十多塊。他向電器行的老板說：「對不起!我下次再來買。」於是把錢包起來，準備帶回去。老板覺得奇怪，便問他：「小朋友，你怎麼會把你的撲滿裡的錢拿來買洗衣機呢?」這小孩回答：「媽媽很辛苦，每天要洗很多衣服，賺錢給我們吃飯、繳學費用。」

Thank you for your help." And so he took his money and prepared[16] to leave the store.

The owner, seeing Bryan's sad face, said, "My young friend, may I ask why you're thinking of buying a washing machine?

Bryan answered softly, "Because my mother works very hard every day. She has too much laundry[17] to do...my sister and I wanted to help her out, and we thought that getting her a washing machine would help her most."

The owner replied, "I see. I'm sorry that you don't have enough money. But, can you please tell me where you live?"

Without[18] thinking much of it, Bryan gave their home address to the man, then left the store and headed home.

A week later, there was a delivery[19] made to their home, it was the owner of the appliance store. He had come with a big washing machine. Mary, caught by surprise[20], said, "I think you have the wrong address. We didn't buy this."

VOCABULARY

16. prepared (v.) 準備
17. laundry (n.) 待洗的衣物
18. without (prep.) 沒有
19. delivery (n.) 運送；遞送
20. surprise (n.) 驚訝

老板聽了小孩的敘述後，問他住在那裡，小孩天真童稚，沒多想什麼便告訴老板地址。小孩回到家後，沒有多久，電器行的老板送來一台更大的洗衣機給這個小朋友。媽媽驚訝地說：「我們哪裡有能力買這台洗衣機呢?」老板告訴她：「不用妳買，是送給妳們的。」

The owner replied, "You're right, you didn't buy it...this is a gift for you."

In complete shock[21], Mary said, "But...how... we cannot accept this."

The owner explained to Mary what happened, then he took out an envelope and said, "This is for your son. On that day, he inspired[22] me to name my new model of washing machine 'Happy Mom.' Please accept this two thousand dollars as payment for giving me a great idea!"

Mary, even more shocked, replied, "No... we cannot take your money."

The owner insisted[23] and said, "If your son had never come to the store and expressed[24] his care for you, I wouldn't have thought of the name. So please accept[25] it, because since then, many customers have ordered this new model from me. This money is the least I can do for him. And the washing machine is that new model too. Please accept my gifts."

不但如此，老板還拿了二十萬塊交給這位媽媽，並且說：「因為妳的小孩給我一個靈感，以後我的洗衣機可以叫做『媽媽樂』，這個名稱會為我賺進很多錢。等於是一種智慧財產，感謝他給我這個啟示，讓我表達我一點心意。」

This story reflects the idea of building a Pure Land on Earth or, in Buddhist terms, the Saha World[26]. In Buddhism, the word Saha means "to bear" or "to endure[27]." In other words, it is a world in which people must endure suffering. It is a world in contrast with a Pure Land. The Saha World is an impure land spoiled by earthly desires and illusions[28]. The question is, how do we turn this Saha World into a Pure Land? In the Buddhist sutras, "Pure Land" means to "purify the land." It means taking action to improve the environment and build a better world and society.

In this story, the love of a caring mother, trying her best to provide her kids with a better life, means she is like a bodhisattva who takes action to transform a humble home into a Pure Land for her children. The son and daughter also acted by saving money to provide a washing machine for their mother. This story demonstrates that the true heritage[29] of Buddhism is found in the willing spirit to transform the world we live in for the better.

At the end of the story, the owner's generosity embodies[30] a wonderful world. His offerings turn the

VOCABULARY

26. Saha World (n.) 娑婆世界
27. endure (v.) 忍耐；容忍
28. illusions (n.) 錯覺；幻想
29. heritage (n.) 遺產
30. embodies (v.) 體現

母親的慈愛，兒女的孝順，老板喜捨，構成一幅人間淨土的景況。當年佛陀以足趾按地，對舍利弗尊者說：「舍利弗！你看！這就是我的世界。」即時三千大千世界，無量珠寶，無量莊嚴，大地金色，整個世界都變成清淨莊嚴的國土。

拂拭心地久積的塵染，睜開千年未開的慧眼，以慈悲對待，以慧心觸摸，你也能看到這個世界的清淨莊嚴。

family's poor situation into a Pure Land overflowing with joy. If we can spread loving-kindness to all, such as when we offer prayers for world peace and the happiness of people, then we are making the Saha World itself into a Pure Land.

When you move forward with this purpose, you are, in the words of a sutra, "propagating³¹ the Law, teaching and changing this Saha World." Buddhists carry out the practices³² of a bodhisattva³³ as emissaries³⁴ of the Buddha. "Let us make our community, our country, and the whole world shine brightly as the Land of Eternally Tranquil Light³⁵."

VOCABULARY

31. propagating (v.) 傳播
32. practices (n.) 實踐
33. bodhisattva (n.) 菩薩
34. emissaries (n.) 使者
35. Land of Eternally Tranquil Light (n.) 常寂光土

Dharma Words by Venerable Master Hsing Yun

By helping each other, every place becomes a paradise;
By respecting neighbors, every place becomes a Pure Land.
Paradise is in my home. The Pure Land is in my mind.

星雲大師法語

人我相助，處處天堂，
鄰里相敬，處處淨土。
天堂在我家中，淨土在我心中。

notes

11

A Loving Son

兒子最好

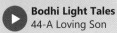

Bodhi Light Tales
44-A Loving Son

Once upon a time, there was a married woman named Leah. When she was young, she enjoyed going to the casino[1] to play card games. Over time, she became addicted[2], and her daily meetings with friends at the casino became her routine. After she got married, Leah persisted[3] with her addiction.

As a housewife, Leah was barely at home with her husband and son, nor did she ever do household chores. One night, after finishing dinner, Leah said to her husband, "I am off to the casino again. Wish me luck... I hope I win the jackpot!"

Looking troubled, her husband grunted[4] and replied, "You always go to the casino! Why can't you just stay home for once and spend time with Joe and me?"

Soon enough, the two began to argue and started yelling at each other. Leah could take no more and so she stormed out[5] of the house, leaving her husband to look after their ten-year-old son.

VOCABULARY

1. casino (n.) 賭場
2. addicted (adj.) 癡迷的；上癮的
3. persisted (v.) 持續
4. grunted (v.) 發出哼聲
5. stormed out (v.) 衝出去

有一個婦人，年輕時就歡喜打牌，幾乎到了一天不打牌，日子就不能過的痴狂地步。一個家庭主婦不在家裡相夫教子、管理家務，吃過飯後就跑出去打牌，每天晨昏顛倒賴在牌桌上，不但浪費時間，有損身體健康，置家庭於不顧更是不當，尤其十賭九輸的牌運，對一個經濟困難的家庭，接踵而來的惡果，真是不堪設想。

On arriving at the casino, Leah was greeted by her usual gaming friends. "Hey, Leah! Ready for a big night?!" said one of them.

"Yes of course! My day wouldn't be complete without seeing you ladies," Leah replied.

As the night wore on, Leah thought back to the argument[6] she had had with her husband and began feeling guilty[7].

She thought to herself, "Maybe I should start heading home, and spend time with my family."

However, Leah was distracted[8] by her friends who called her out and pressured her to make yet another bet. The next thing she knew, Leah woke up the next morning to find herself sprawled[9] on the casino floor. She picked up her phone and saw the many missed calls and messages from her husband. There was even a voicemail[10] from her son, saying how much he missed her.

All this made Leah realize, "Maybe last night

VOCABULARY

6. argument (n.) 爭論；爭吵
7. guilty (adj.) 內疚的；愧疚的
8. distracted (adj.) 分心的
9. sprawled (v.) 伸開四肢躺
10. voicemail (n.) 語音信箱

但是嗜賭如命的婦人，就算家境陷入窘境，還是無法抗拒打牌的衝動與欲望，天天跑去打牌，也天天輸錢回家。

was a waste of time, and always sleeping late isn't great for my health either. I'm so uncaring for ignoring[11] my family."

The family was already having trouble making ends meet[12], and the odds[13] of her winning at the casino were very low. Despite this and the thought of her family sinking further into financial debt, Leah's addiction was such that she could not resist[14] the urge to gamble at the casino. As a result of her addiction, she came home every day having lost even more of the family's savings.

One afternoon, after picking up her son Joe from school, Leah yet again couldn't help herself and headed for the casino. Joe, being young and innocent[15], could only follow. But, Leah had forgotten that today was Joe's birthday.

After a few bets, Joe said to his mother, "Can we please go home now?"

Seeing Joe's pleading, Leah decided to end her night at the casino early.

On the way home, Leah remembered

VOCABULARY

11. ignoring (v.) 不理睬；忽視
12. make ends meet (phrase) 使收支平衡
13. odds (n.) 機率
14. resist (v.) 按捺；忍住
15. innocent (adj.) 天真的

這個婦人每次去賭場，總會帶著十歲大的小兒子同行。有一次她又賭輸了，從賭場要回家的途中，突然想起家中的米缸沒有米了，要想買一點米回去煮晚餐，但是掏掏口袋，卻發現自己身上竟然連一塊錢也沒有。

正當她感到為難的時候，小兒子從身上掏出幾塊錢來，遞到她的手上。婦人看了，驚訝地問：「你怎麼會有錢呢？」

that they were out of groceries, and so took a detour[16] to the supermarket. As they passed a cake shop, Joe stopped and stared at the many delicious cakes on display.

He quickly asked, "Mom, can we please buy a cake?"

Leah thought for a second, realized[17] it was Joe's birthday, and quickly replied, "Oh my little angel, it's your birthday today! I'm so sorry, of course we should get you a cake!"

Inside the cake shop, Joe immediately pointed at the chocolate mud cake. Leah knew it was his favorite cake and was about to order it. But as she reached into her pocket, she realized she had not even a single coin to spare[18]. Feeling ashamed[19], she looked at Joe. Suddenly, out of nowhere, Joe pulled out money from his pocket and gave it to his mother.

Astonished[20] at what just happened, Leah asked Joe, "Where did this money come from?"

Joe replied, "Oh, I've been saving. The money I got for Chinese New Year, money for my breakfast, and also the money Dad gave me to buy cookies."

VOCABULARY

16. detour (n.) 繞行的路；繞道
17. realized (v.) 意識到
18. spare (v.) 剩下；多餘
19. ashamed (adj.) 羞愧的；不好意思的
20. astonished (adj.) 感到驚訝的

小兒子說：「哦！我把過年的壓歲錢、上學買早餐的錢，還有上回買燒餅的錢都留下來了啊！」

這時候婦人才警覺到自己已經很久沒有關心孩子，含著淚接下小兒子存下的錢後，便牽著他的手一起去買米。

It was at this moment that Leah realized she had been a bad mother, neglecting[21] her son all this time while she was out gambling. With tears streaming[22] down her face, she took the money that Joe had thoughtfully saved up and handed it to the cashier.

Seeing first-hand[23] how thoughtful and considerate her son was, Leah's cold, inconsiderate[24] heart finally melted[25].

When they got home, she hugged Joe and said "You are such a great son! I am so sorry for not spending more time with you. I promise to

VOCABULARY

21. neglecting (v.) 忽視；疏忽
22. streaming (v.) 流出
23. first-hand (adv.) 親身
24. inconsiderate (adj.) 不顧別人的
25. melted (v.) 軟化

　　面對這樣貼心、懂事的小孩，母親的鐵石心腸終於軟化，回到家裡，她抱著兒子說：「兒子，你最好了！」從此，她下定決心戒掉牌癮，革除惡習，重新做人。

be a better mother, just as you have been such a loving son in helping the family."

From then on, Leah was resolved[26] to quit her gambling addiction, undo her bad habits, and start afresh.

This story highlights[27] that a touched heart is the most beautiful thing in this world. If we think about it, are we not touched by the love our parents have given us? Are we not touched by our teachers' sincere efforts in teaching us? Are we not touched by the blessings[28] that this world has given us?

If we are touched by our surroundings, we will live a life of happiness, and shall never give up on our efforts. We will live in harmony with others and spread joy to all around us.

We should not only be grateful[29] for the kind words and thoughtful actions we receive from others, but we should pay it forward by speaking good words and doing good deeds[30] so that those around us will feel touched. If each and every one of us can do this, the world will be a better place, for being moved is most beautiful.

VOCABULARY

26. resolved (adj.)
    下定決心的；堅定的；堅決的

27. highlights (v.) 強調

28. blessings (n.) 祝福；幸事

29. grateful (adj.) 感激的；表示感謝的

30. deeds (n.) 事情；行為

感動的世界很美好。想想，難道父母給我們的愛，我都不感動嗎？老師對我們的苦心教學，我都不感動嗎？我們接受世間多少的恩惠，一點都不感動嗎？甚至不只對於別人所說的話、所做的事，要有感動，自己每天所說的話、所做的事，也要讓人感動，互相感動來、感動去，就是一個感動的世界了。

Dharma Words by Venerable Master Hsing Yun

Being deeply moved is an important part of practice.
We must be sensitive and grateful to the kind words
and the kind deeds we come across in our daily lives.
We must also touch others with compassion,
tolerance, modesty, and diligence.
If everyone can be moved, the world will be a great Pure Land.

星雲大師法語

感動是人間修行的重要法門，
我們每天不但應該對於別人所作的善事，
所說的好話心存感動，
自己也要以慈悲、忍耐、謙遜、勤勞等美德來感動他人。
如果能夠做到自他感動，佛國淨土即在眼前。

12

On Generosity

A Night Out

沙彌夜遊

Bodhi Light Tales
47-A Night Out

Once upon a time, there lived a Zen Master named Sengai. He was a Japanese monk from the Rinzai[1] school. Though the Rinzai school is known for its complex and difficult teachings, Master Sengai tried to make it approachable[2] and understandable to the people. As a result, he was known for his controversial[3] teachings and writings.

Master Sengai had many novice monks as disciples, and many were young and still enjoyed having fun. Often, after the evening Dharma service, some of the novice monks would sneak[4] out of the monastery. They would leave through the back garden and climb over the stone walls. As they very much enjoyed their time outside, they would often return just before midnight.

One night, while on patrol[5], Master Sengai walked through the back garden and noticed there was a chair placed against the wall. He immediately knew that someone had sneaked out. Quietly, he removed the chair, stood in its place, and simply waited there.

VOCABULARY

1. Rinzai (n.) 日本臨濟宗
2. approachable (adj.) 容易親近的
3. controversial (adj.) 有爭議的；引起爭論的
4. sneak (v.) 偷偷地走
5. patrol (n.) 巡邏；巡視

仙崖禪師收了許多沙彌作弟子，這些沙彌因為年幼，玩心重，經常在做完晚課以後，偷偷地翻牆出去遊玩，直到半夜才回來。

有一天晚上，仙崖禪師走到後院，刻意把沙彌放在牆角藉以攀爬的高腳凳拿走，自己站在那裡。過了初更，沙彌從牆頭爬下來，慣性地踩在高腳凳的位置上，準備跳下。「咦！怎麼軟綿綿的？」

As the time neared midnight, Master Sengai heard whispers[6] from afar. As the whispers came closer to the wall of the monastery, Master Sengai recognized the voices as his novice monks, returning to the monastery after their evening outing. The first novice monk climbed carefully up the wall. Familiar with his nightly routine, he knew exactly where to lower himself and was expecting to place his feet on the chair he had left there earlier that night.

The novice monk thought to himself, "Hmmm...something feels rather odd today, why does the chair feel soft and plushy[7]? "Now very curious, he looked down, "Oh no! It's our Master's shoulders!" He blurted out[8] in shock.

One by one, the novice monks climbed down from the wall, this time relying on their Master's shoulders to safely get down. Looking and feeling ashamed[9], they all stood in front of their master, utterly[10] speechless. Master Sengai looked at each one of them with compassion and said, "It's late, let's hurry back and get warm

---

VOCABULARY

6. whispers (n.) 颯颯的聲音
7. plushy (adj.) 毛絨絨的
8. blurted out (phrase) 脫口說出
9. ashamed (adj.) 羞愧的；慚愧的
10. utterly (adv.) 完全地

沙彌心生疑惑，再往下一看，不得了，竟然是仙崖禪師的肩膀。沙彌不知所措，仙崖禪師卻以關愛的眼神，拍拍沙彌的肩膀，說道：「孩子！夜深了，小心著涼，趕快回去加件衣裳吧！」從此以後，寺院裡再沒有人出去夜遊；對這件事，仙崖禪師也從未和別人提起。

before you all catch a cold."

From then on, none of the novice monks dared to sneak out of the monastery again. Aside from telling the novice monks to hurry back in, Master Sengai never spoke to them of the incident again, nor did he scold the novice monks for their mischief[11].

This story highlights that we can teach someone lessons with compassion and wisdom. In this story, Master Sengai did not admonish[12] the novice monks for sneaking out. Instead, he acted with compassion.

Knowing how the novice monks would have reacted if he had scolded[13] them. And his response of "It's late, let's hurry back and get warm before you all catch a cold" was far more effective[14] in teaching these novice monks the lesson they needed. Had he told them off and punished them, it may not have been as effective. This is a good reminder for parents and teachers about the ways we should teach our children.

In the Chan school, there is a rather profound[15] way of teaching, which is "not to speak too plainly." As parents, this can be a good way to educate children.

VOCABULARY

11. mischief (n.) 惡作劇；淘氣
12. admonish (v.) 訓誡；責備
13. scolded (v.) 責罵；責備
14. effective (adj.) 有效的
15. profound (adj.) 深奧的

禪門的「不說破」是很高深的教育方法。現代父母教育兒女也當如此，要為孩子留尊嚴，顧自尊。動不動就罵孩子「沒出息」、「你沒用」，不僅罵得小孩子失去尊嚴，自卑心起，也容易導致思想與行為產生偏差；老師教育學生，也要替學生留顏面，「你不聰明」、「你這麼笨」、「真沒有出息」的責備、數落，學生聽久了，就難以奮起飛揚，也容易墮落了。

It is important to think about the self-esteem and dignity[16] of children. We shouldn't yell at them, or lecture them with hurtful and harsh speech like "You're pathetic!" or "You're useless!" If we say such harsh words, the children are left with no dignity and may even nurture feelings of resentment[17] and incompetence[18]. This can also surely affect their self-esteem[19] and future behavior. Likewise, as teachers, students also need to be respected. Hence, such hurtful remarks like "You're not smart enough," or "You're so stupid," or "You'll never be any good," are harmful in the long run, as students would lose confidence and struggle to improve.

For children to have self-respect and self-confidence, we must respect their dignity and self-esteem, have faith in them, as well as love and care for them. This will help them in their process of learning and growing, and they will definitely improve. Education is very important in our lives. However, the method used in educating is equally important. Sometimes, an unintended word or action may have a huge impact on someone's mind and well-being[20].

VOCABULARY

16. dignity (n.) 尊嚴

17. resentment (n.) 憤怒；怨恨

18. incompetence (n.) 無能力

19. self-esteem (n.) 自尊

20. well-being (n.) 幸福；安康

要孩子自尊自重，先要給他自尊、信心與關愛，孩子的學習過程自會展現好的成果，進步也快。教育是人生大事，無心一句話、一個動作，對於孩子身心的影響巨大，怎可不慎。其實，孩子的行為必有深藏心底的原因，教育不應只在表象上琢磨，而是關心背後的動機，才是根本之道。仙崖禪師一句「夜深露重，小心著涼」，含藏的悲智，天下父母與老師可會得了？

How can we not exercise caution about this?

In reality, there are always deep-down[21] reasons behind the behavior of our children. Fundamentally, educating them will require more than just scraping the surface[22], but we must first ask and consider what are their true, and often hidden[23] intentions[24].

VOCABULARY

21. deep-down (adj.) 在內心深處的
22. scraping the surface (phrase) 僅觸及問題的表面
23. hidden (adj.) 不為人知的；隱藏的
24. intentions (n.) 意圖

Dharma Words by Venerable Master Hsing Yun

Value people for their knowledge,
not their appearance.
Value people for their will and aspirations,
not their knowledge.

星雲大師法語

從長相來判斷一個人，
不如從所學來判斷一個人。
從所學來判斷一個人，
不如從心志來判斷一個人。

notes

13

On Generosity

A Boy's Offering

小兒施土

Bodhi Light Tales
49- A Boy's Offering

Scan me to listen!

掃我，聆聽故事!

Once upon a time, the Buddha and his disciple Ananda traveled to Sravasti, a city in ancient India. The Buddha often walked between places, teaching and connecting with the people. This time, the Buddha and Ananda were there for alms offering[1], which is a form of cultivation[2] where the monastics went door-to-door to beg for food. This was a common practice in the Buddha's time. It was an opportunity[3] for the community to practice generosity[4] by making offerings and, in return, they learned the Buddha's teachings.

As the Buddha and Ananda went around for the alms offering, they saw a group of children playing on the side of the road. The children were using dirt to build castles, houses, and they even made treasures and crops that were kept in the houses.

A little boy named Jaya, very focused on fashioning[5] crops out of dirt, looked up and saw the Buddha slowly walking closer. Immediately, he thought to himself, "I wish to make an

VOCABULARY

1. alms offering (n.) 托缽乞食
2. cultivation (n.) 修行
3. opportunity (n.) 機遇；時機；機會
4. generosity (n.) 布施
5. fashioning (v.) 製造；塑造

　　有一次，佛陀和阿難入舍衛城托缽乞食，看到一群兒童在路邊玩耍嬉戲，以泥沙建造宮殿、倉庫，及儲藏在倉庫內的財寶、五穀。

offering to the Buddha." With his bare[6] hands, he grabbed[7] a handful of the crops he had made and walked towards the Buddha.

As Jaya was about to make his offering, he realized he was not tall enough.

So, he asked his friend next to him, "Will you let me stand on your shoulders, so I can make an offering to the Buddha?"

His friend happily replied,

"Okay, go ahead!"

Jaya then carefully stood on his shoulders, balancing himself before he reached out and made the offering to the Buddha.

Seeing Jaya's efforts, the Buddha stretched[8] out his hands and happily accepted the offering. Ananda, observing what had just happened, was very confused[9].

He thought to himself, "Offering dirt to the Buddha is rather disrespectful[10]. How can one even think of offering such a thing to the

VOCABULARY

6. bare (adj.) 空的
7. grabbed (v.) 抓取
8. stretched (v.) 伸展；張開
9. confused (adj.) 困惑的
10. disrespectful (adj.)
    失禮的；無禮的

這時候，有一個小孩遠遠地看見佛陀緩緩走來，布施心油然生起，立刻從倉庫中取出一把穀物，準備供養給佛陀。但是由於他的身形矮小，不及佛陀的高大，便拜託另外一個小孩，說：「讓我站在你的肩膀上，好將穀物奉獻給佛陀。」那個小孩一聽，歡喜地說：「好啊！」就這樣，他得以順利將穀物供養給佛陀。

Buddha?"

As they continued to make their way around the neighborhood, begging for alms, this question continued to circle in Ananda's mind. When they returned to the monastery, Ananda finally asked, "Buddha, while we were on our alms rounds today, why did you accept the offering made of dirt from that boy?"

The Buddha answered, "Ananda, this boy's offering came from his heart, we should not look down on him. He offered the dirt to me with a pure mind without discrimination[11]. A hundred years after my death, that boy will reap[12] the benefit of the sincere offering he made today. He will become a King called Ashoka, and the other boy that helped him shall be his closest minister. In the future, they will be the leaders of this country, they will care for the people, and they will honor[13] and respect the Buddha, Dharma, and Sangha. Moreover, they will share my relics[14] and build many pagodas all over this country to preserve[15] my teachings."

VOCABULARY

11. discrimination (n.) 歧視
12. reap (v.) 收穫；獲得
13. honor (v.) 向…致敬
14. relics (n.) 舍利
15. preserve (v.) 維護；保存

當時，佛陀伸出雙手，歡喜接受供養，這一幕看在阿難的眼裡，心裡很是不解：為什麼佛陀要接受泥沙做成的穀物呢？回到了精舍，阿難請問佛陀：「佛陀，為什您要接受以沙土做成的穀物呢？」

This story highlights that what we reap depends on how we sow[16]. Whether we attract wholesome[17] or unwholesome karma will depend on our minds. When Jaya wanted to make an offering to the Buddha, it came from a pure heart. At that moment, the dirt in Jaya's hands was not dirt, it was what he made. In his mind, all he could think about was making an offering to the Buddha. This also teaches us to not be idle in waiting for the right moment. Sometimes, we focus only on how much or how large what we want to offer is. However, it is most important that we are aware of our true intentions in the act of giving.

For example, the purpose of donating one million dollars may be driven by wanting recognition[18], demanding to have our name engraved on a plaque[19] or the wall of benefactors[20]. However, someone may simply wish to donate a loaf of bread, in the hope that those who receive it can feel a sense of joy. In this scenario, the merits of donating the bread far surpass those of donating a million dollars. While there is a difference between one million dollars and a loaf of bread, the intention behind the donations differs even

VOCABULARY

16. sow (v.) 播種
17. wholesome (adj.) 善的
18. recognition (n.) 讚賞；認可
19. plaque (n.) 銘牌
20. benefactors (n.) 捐助者

佛陀就說了：「阿難，這個小孩的布施是沒有分別心的，不可以輕視！他以泥沙供養我，在我涅槃後的一百年間，將會得到做大國王的福報，名叫阿育，而另外一個兒童，也將做侍臣來擁護他。未來他們將領導這個人世間所有的國土，興隆三寶，遍布我的舍利，並且啟建八萬四千塔。」

more. As a result, this means that there will also be a vast[21] difference in the merits gained. In other words, we must be clear of our intentions, as wholesome, true intentions will lead us on a path[22] toward greatness.

21. vast (adj.) 巨大的;廣大的
22. path (n.) 道路

所謂「心田事不同,功德分勝劣」,你捐獻一百萬元,只是希望在牆上鐫刻自己的名字,而他捐獻一個麵包,是希望所有吃到的人都能感到歡喜,功德可說勝過一百萬元的布施。在事相上,一百萬元和一個麵包雖有差別,但是因為發心不同,功德也就有大小之分了。

Dharma Words by Venerable Master Hsing Yun

There is no merit in giving millions
when you wish for a reward.
A grain of rice given without attachment
is the same as a thousand bushels.

星雲大師法語

施捨者，內不見己，外不見人，
中不見物，雖粒米之施，當如萬鍾之粟。
利人者，望人回報，計己之能，
美施之物，雖百億金銀，難比一文之值。

notes

14

On Generosity

Offering the Light

貧女一燈

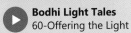
Bodhi Light Tales
60-Offering the Light

Once upon a time, there lived a lady named Nina. Her family was very poor and they struggled to put food on the table. Her father had left them when she was a baby. Despite living in such dire[1] circumstances, Nina was strong-willed[2] and had a pure heart. She admired[3] the Buddha for his compassion and wisdom, and wished to follow him and his practices.

One day, Nina was on her way to the market and walked past a temple. She saw people inside the temple paying respect to the Buddha, making offerings of food and candles. She thought to herself, "I wish I could make a lamp offering to the Buddha, but I have nothing to give. The Buddha's teachings have helped so many people, if only I could practice and follow in his footsteps." With that aspiration[4] lingering[5] in her mind, Nina went home.

On the way home, she walked past a bridge and heard the water flowing from the small river. As she looked down at the water, she noticed her own reflection. In her reflection on the water's

VOCABULARY

1. dire (adj.) 悲慘的
2. strong-willed (adj.) 意志堅強的
3. admired (v.) 欽佩
4. aspiration (n.) 願心
5. lingering (v.) 徘徊

有一個小女孩，家裡非常貧窮，三餐難以為繼。有一天，她經過一間寺院，看到寺院裡有很多人在拜佛、供齋、點燈，心裡就想：唉！真慚愧，自己實在沒有力量，要是有錢的話，就能在佛前點上一盞燈了。

surface, she saw her long hair and immediately thought, "I know! I'll cut my hair off and sell it. Then I'll have money to buy an oil lamp, and I can make a lamp offering to the Buddha." Right there and then, Nina cut off her hair, sold it, and used the money she earned to buy an oil lamp.

With her newly bought lamp, Nina went to the temple, walked into the Main Shrine, and offered it to the Buddha. In good faith, she knelt in front of the Buddha and prayed, before carefully placing the lamp in front of him.

On the altar, hundreds of lavish[6] and costly candles were lit, illuminating[7] the whole shrine. In contrast, Nina's lamp was small, plain, and modest[8].

"Excuse me, make way there!" said a wealthy woman, a benefactor[9] who had supported the temple for many years and had offered all those expensive lamps. She looked at all the lamps on the altar, and with no hesitation[10] began complaining, "Who lit this cheap oil lamp? How can it be an offering to the Buddha? Its place

---

VOCABULARY

6. lavish (adj.) 奢華的；豪華的
7. illuminating (v.) 照亮
8. modest (adj.) 不貴的；樸素的
9. benefactor (n.) 捐助者
10. hesitation (n.) 猶豫

帶著這樣的渴望，貧女失落地回家去了。途中，她經過一座橋，橋下涓涓的細流，倒映出她的影子。貧女從水面上看到自己的一頭黑髮時，忽然心生一念：有了！把頭髮剪下來，拿去賣錢，買了油就可以點燈了！

is outside, not here in front of the Buddha. It disgraces[11] the setting of the shrine."

A novice monk heard the heartless[12] words from the wealthy woman and said, "If you knew the story of the poor lady who offered the lamp you speak of, you would not look down on her offering."

Looking over and pointing at Nina, the novice monk continued, "This lamp was offered by Nina. She cut off and sold her hair, and bought that lamp with all the money she had to make this offering to the Buddha. This offering is everything that Nina has, body, heart, and mind."

Just as the novice monk finished speaking, a huge gust[13] of wind suddenly swept[14] across the altar and extinguished[15] all the expensive candles offered by the benefactor. In this new darkness, only Nina's lamp remained shining brightly.

Seeing what just happened, the wealthy benefactor was shocked and moved.

VOCABULARY

11. disgraces (v.) 使恥辱
12. heartless (adj.) 無情的
13. gust (n.) 一陣
14. swept (v.) 捲走；席捲
15. extinguished (v.) 熄滅

當貧女再度來到寺院的時候，她以最虔誠的心，在佛前點了一盞油燈。但是一盞小小的油燈，在滿室光明燦爛的油燈前，顯得特別簡陋，一位家財萬貫的大施主看了，不禁責罵道：「這一盞粗陋的油燈是誰點的？怎麼可以供在佛前，破壞這麼莊嚴的氣氛呢？」

知客師聽到大施主責怪的言詞，就說了：「大施主！你不可以責怪這盞燈的主人！這是貧窮的女施主阿照變賣自己的頭髮，以賣髮所得供養的一盞油燈，她是以全副身心來供養這盞燈的啊！」

She approached[16] Nina carefully and said, "My dear, I was wrong, please forgive my rudeness[17]. I truly admire your inner beauty and compassion. Is there anything I can do for you?"

Nina, taken by surprise, simply shook her head and remained silent.

The benefactor continued, "What are your aspirations? What is it that you wish for? My own wish is to help you."

Nina replied softly, "I am touched by the Buddha's teachings, so I wish to follow the Buddha's path and practice."

Upon hearing Nina's wishes, the benefactor replied, "That is the noblest aspiration. Very well, I will build a nunnery[18] for you. And you won't have to worry about anything, I will have all essentials[19] delivered to you daily, so you can focus on your practice."

Before long, the nunnery was built and Nina moved in, diligently[20] practicing the teachings of the Buddha each day.

On a particularly cold winter evening, a

VOCABULARY

16. approached (v.) 靠近
17. rudeness (n.) 無禮
18. nunnery (n.) 尼寺；尼庵
19. essentials (n.) 必需品
20. diligently (adv.) 勤奮地

當知客師講完這些話的時候，忽然颳起一陣大風，把這位大施主所供養的幾百盞燈，統統都吹熄了。在一片漆黑當中，只有貧女阿照的那一盞燈，仍然大放光明。

看到這個情景，大施主非常感動，就對阿照說：「妳有什麼心願？我很有錢，能幫助妳完成願望。」沒想到阿照卻淡淡地說：「我只想學佛修行！」大施主一聽，就說：「好！那我就發心為妳建造一間庵堂吧！」

snowstorm swept through the nunnery. Nina was not distracted[21] by the storm, and she continued her practice as usual. But suddenly, Nina's mindful[22] concentration[23] was broken by the sound of something heavy hitting the front door.

She got up, opened the door, and saw an old man lying in the doorway covered in snow. In a heartbeat, Nina was by the man's side, "Are you all right?" she asked.

The old man was too weak to speak, so Nina brought him inside. After making sure he was comfortable, Nina quickly made him a warm cup of tea and helped him settle down. Soon, the old man regained[24] his energy and his wits. He slowly opened his eyes, looked at Nina, and softly said, "Thank you so much."

Nina took care of the old man for a few days. Through their conversations, Nina discovered that this old man was, in fact, her biological[25] father. The old man told her that he had been looking for his lost daughter, as he had always

VOCABULARY

21. distracted (adj.) 分散注意力的
22. mindful (adj.) 覺察的；正念的
23. concentration (n.) 專注；專心
24. regained (v.) 重新獲得
25. biological (adj.) 親生的

某天，在一個大風雪的夜晚，阿照仍然像平常一樣，在庵堂裡精進修行，忽然間，一陣碰撞聲響起。阿照開門一看，竟是一個老人倒臥在門口，好心的阿照一個箭步上前將他救起。進到屋內後，阿照以溫暖的茶飯侍候，悉心照料，很快地，被凍得奄奄一息的老人就甦醒過來了。

felt ashamed of abandoning[26] his family. In life's journey of twists and turns[27], it was Nina's actions that led them to finally be reunited[28] after all these years.

This story teaches us the true meaning behind the practice and act of giving. Offering a single penny does not mean it is a small offering. Likewise, offering thousands of dollars does not mean it is a generous offering.

What matters when giving is our mindset at that precise moment. If our efforts and aspirations when giving are sincere, unbelievably good causes and conditions will follow us, often when least expected.

Just like Nina's lamp offering, a sincere offering led to great merits. Even the strongest wind could not extinguish the flame from Nina's humble offering. If we can leave behind our self-centered[29] ways of living and replace them with compassionate acts of generosity, our good affinities will naturally flourish.

This story also provides insights[30] into the meaning behind offering a lamp, or simply put, making a light offering. Symbolically, we have always

---

VOCABULARY

26. abandoning (v.) 拋棄；離棄
27. twists and turns (phrase) 波折
28. reunited (v.) 使重聚
29. self-centered (adj.) 利己主義的
30. insights (n.) 深刻見解

由於阿照的好心，後來才發現，原來這個老人不是別人，正是她自幼就失散的父親。從此，父女終於團圓了。

seen fire as a source of life. In the darkness, shining a light is the instrument of our vision and bathes our surroundings with an energy that brings hope. For example, sitting around a campfire can provide the perfect atmosphere[31] in which to tell stories that can greatly impact[32] a person's life. Therefore, Nina's sincere light offering to the Buddha was symbolic of the light of life and hope that never fades away[33].

This inspires us to never overlook[34] an opportunity to give, no matter how small it may seem to us or others.

A mind of compassion and sincerity can profoundly[35] move people even through the seemingly smallest of acts. Through giving, we can realize our true power of connecting with and serving others.

VOCABULARY

31. atmosphere (n.) 氣氛
32. impact (v.) 影響
33. fades away (phrase) 逐漸消失
34. overlook (v.) 忽略；忽視
35. profoundly (adv.) 深刻地；極度地

所謂「布施」，一毛錢不一定是少，萬萬千千也不一定是多，一切都要視你的發心如何，只要真心誠意，不可思議的善因好緣就會跟隨而來。如同貧女一燈，其功德之大，就是再大的風，也都無法吹熄。

Dharma Words by Venerable Master Hsing Yun

Practicing generosity without reward is noble.
Practicing generosity without regret is to be praised.

星雲大師法語

無求的布施，端嚴高貴，令人感念。

無悔的布施，身心光明，令人讚美。

notes

15

On Generosity

The Painters

畫師作畫

 Scan me to listen!
掃我，聆聽故事！

Once upon a time, there lived in a kingdom a group of painters. Each had a unique style. Every week, the group would meet and discuss painting techniques[1]. Some were good at outlining shapes, but not at painting in colors. Some were good at coloring, but not sketching[2]. Some were good at sketching bodies, but not hands or feet. Some were good at painting hands and feet, but not facial features[3].

At one gathering, Claude, one of the painters, sighed and said, "I should have been paid for my work."

"What happened?" asked his friend, Vince.

"A merchant asked me to paint for free. He told me he would promote[4] my paintings, and this would raise my profile[5] as an artist. Though I was against it, I didn't say no. In the end, I agreed to five paintings. Before coming here, I met the merchant who said one of my paintings just sold for a lot of money," Claude said.

"That's good! That means people like your paintings," Vince replied.

VOCABULARY

1. techniques (n.) 技術；技巧
2. sketching (v.) 畫素描
3. features (n.) 特徵
4. promote (v.) 推銷；推廣
5. profile (n.) 形象；個人簡介

過去有一群以繪畫為業的畫師，經常聚在一起切磋畫技。他們在繪畫藝術上都各有專精，有的擅於描繪輪廓，但不精於塗抹顏色；有的擅於上色，但不精於素描；有的長於畫身體，但不善於畫手腳；有的長於畫手足，但不善於畫五官。然而，經過一段長時間的聚會研究後，大家不只在各自的專長上有長足的進步，就是在其他繪畫的技巧上，也都突飛猛進。

"Yes... But I'm not making any money," Claude said.

The leader of the group, Jasper, overheard[6] and said, "It's always good for us to gain recognition[7] through our paintings. We always have a choice. If you agreed to paint for free, you knew what that would mean."

Claude replied, "I should have thought it through, I was doubting[8] myself...that my paintings weren't that great."

"As artists, we must have faith in ourselves and our paintings. If you doubt yourself, others will see it and take advantage[9]. You're very talented[10], Claude. Be more confident." Jasper said.

Claude nodded and said, "You're right."

As other painters arrived, Jasper clapped his hands and said to the group, "Shall we begin?" They all took out their painting tools and began their work.

VOCABULARY

6. overheard (v.) 無意中聽到；偶然聽到
7. recognition (n.) 認可
8. doubting (v.) 懷疑
9. advantage (n.) 利益
10. talented (adj.)
    有才能的；能幹的；技藝高超的

當時，有一位國王一心想找人為他畫一幅肖像，聽聞國中有這麼一群畫師，便喚人把他們請入宮中。一時之間，這群畫師齊聚一堂。這時候，國王指著一張畫布，對大家說：「各位畫師！今天找你們來，是想請你們在這塊布上為我畫一幅肖像，如果你們能夠畫得令我滿意，必定會有重賞！」

Since joining the group, many had made great progress[11] not only in their own style but also by learning different techniques from one another.

One day, the King wanted someone to paint his portrait. Word of this painters group reached him and he asked his minister to invite them to the palace.

When the group arrived, the King greeted them and said, "Welcome! I invited you all today because I want you to paint my portrait[12]. If the portrait pleases me, you shall all be rewarded[13]!"

The painters were thrilled[14] at this opportunity. Immediately, they took their positions and began. Each played to their strengths[15], some started to draw outlines,

VOCABULARY

11. progress (n.) 進步；進展
12. portrait (n.) 肖像；人像
13. rewarded (v.) 報償；獎賞
14. thrilled (adj.) 激動的
15. strengths (n.) 強項

國王話一說完，所有畫師便各就各位，開始在這塊布上揮灑。只見畫師們各自發揮所長，有的開始構圖，有的屏氣凝神地勾勒著五官，有的專心地畫手腳，有的仔細地上顏色……但是，就在作品即將完成的那一刻，大家赫然發現，擅長畫身體的畫師沒有到。正當不知如何是好的時候，有人提議說：「我們不妨一起合力來完成這幅畫吧！」

others focused on the facial features or began drawing hands and feet, and some carefully used colors. As they were close to finishing, they realized that Vince, usually very good at drawing the human body, was nowhere to be seen.

When the King saw that his portrait was missing a body, he was furious[16] and said, "How could you paint me without a body?! If no one fixes this, all of you will be executed[17]!"

Panicking[18], Claude complained, "It's Vince's fault[19] for not being here! Now we're in trouble!"

Jasper gathered everyone and said, "OK, this is a test of our creativity[20]. If we truly work as a team, we can finish this portrait. Vince has shared his techniques with us before, so let's all work together to finish it!"

The others nodded in agreement. They picked up their paintbrushes and worked

---

VOCABULARY

16. furious (adj.)
    極其生氣的；怒不可遏的

17. executed (v.) 處死

18. panicking (v.) 恐慌；驚慌失措

19. fault (n.) 過錯；過失

20. creativity (n.) 創造力；創意

在大夥兒通力合作下，好不容易，國王的肖像畫終於完成了。呈獻給國王的那一刻，只見國王眉開眼笑，頻頻誇讚說：「畫得太好了！畫得太好了！」畫師們才終於鬆了一口氣。

together to complete the body. Working as a group, the King's portrait was finally completed. When the King saw his finished portrait, he exclaimed[21], "Wonderful! Excellent painting!"

The painters all cheered[22] with relief[23]. As promised, the King made sure to give the group a huge reward.

This story highlights the importance of teamwork[24]. Everything in this world is only possible due to many conditions coming together. For instance, a building requires steel[25], cement, bricks, and other materials. A soccer game requires the effort of each player, in different positions, playing their best to win the game.

In this story, the painters were able to complete the portrait because they were willing to work as a team. More importantly, they were willing to share their skills and learn from each other. One person's wisdom

VOCABULARY

21. exclaimed (v.) 呼喊
22. cheered (v.) 歡呼
23. relief (n.) 寬慰；鬆一口氣
24. teamwork (n.) 團隊合作
25. steel (n.) 鋼鐵

世間一切都是因緣和合而成的，你看一棟房子，尚且需要鋼筋、水泥、磚瓦等建材才能完成；一場球賽，也必須隊員們同心協力才能獲勝。因此，每個人都不能小看自己在團體裡的重要性。中國有句俗諺：「三個臭皮匠，勝過一個諸葛亮。」 一個人的智慧終究是有限的，唯有集合眾人的力量，彼此互助合作，才能共同成就一番事業。

is limited, but if we combine everyone's strengths, then success lies ahead. No one should underestimate[26] their worth[27] and contributions[28] to a group.

As the saying goes, "Two heads are better than one." Opportunities are limitless[29] if we are willing to let go of our ego[30] and team up with others.

VOCABULARY

26. underestimate (v.) 低估；看輕
27. worth (n.) 價值
28. contributions (n.) 貢獻；奉獻
29. limitless (adj.) 無限的
30. ego (n.) 自我中心；自尊心

Dharma Words by Venerable Master Hsing Yun

Unity means working together;
Working together leads to unity.
Harmony means respecting others;
Respect leads to harmony.

星雲大師法語

團結就是互相分工合作，合作才能團結。
融和就是彼此平等尊重，尊重才能融和。

16

On Generosity

Praying for Wealth

求富

Bodhi Light Tales
70-Praying for Wealth

Once upon a time, there lived two brothers in a small town. The eldest was called Ian and the younger brother was called Lucas. After their parents retired[1], Ian and Lucas took care of the farm. The life of the family had always been difficult.

One day, Ian said to Lucas, "Did you hear about Ken?"

"Our neighbor? What happened?" Lucas asked.

"He got rich. I heard that not long ago, he began praying[2] to the Heavenly God[3]. Now, he no longer needs to work," Ian said.

"Are you sure?" Lucas replied with a frown.

"Yes, I'm sure. We've always wanted an easier and better life, I think we should pray as he did," Ian said.

Lucas grunted[4] and replied, "I'm not so sure, it sounds too good to be true. Even if it is true, I think someone should still cultivate[5] our field."

"I have an idea, how about you continue to

VOCABULARY

1. retired (v.) 退休；退職
2. praying (v.) 祈禱
3. Heavenly God (n.) 天神
4. grunted (v.) 咕噥；發出哼聲
5. cultivate (v.) 耕作；栽培；種植

過去有兄弟兩人，過著十分困苦的日子。為了改善生活，有一天他們決定由哥哥負責向天神祈禱，希望能夠發財富貴，弟弟則負責耕地種田，以求農作物豐收。

work in the field and I will pray for the both of us?" Ian proposed.

Lucas was still hesitant[6], but Ian insisted[7], "Come on! It's worth trying. I'm already excited just thinking about buying a new house."

Lucas nodded and said, "Ok. I'll focus on the field."

"It's a deal!" Ian said with a big grin.

From that day on, Ian prayed diligently. Day and night he prayed, "Dear Heavenly God, our family begs for your kindness, please give us wealth and honor[8]. We promise to repay you!"

One month passed, and Ian was still praying without any sign of success.

However, Ian's diligence[9] and sincerity touched the Heavenly God, who decided to help. The Heavenly God disguised[10] himself as Lucas and met with Ian.

When Ian saw Lucas, he asked, "Why are you here? You're supposed to be working on the field?"

"I feel I should follow your lead and pray

VOCABULARY

6. hesitant (adj.) 遲疑的
7. insisted (v.) 堅持
8. honor (n.) 名譽
9. diligence (n.) 勤奮
10. disguised (v.) 偽裝；化裝

從那天開始，哥哥日夜精進，不斷地禮拜毗沙門天神，期望能夠獲得大富大貴。經過一段時日，一天，毗沙門天神化身成弟弟的模樣，來到哥哥身邊。哥哥看到弟弟忽然跑來，就問：「你不去工作，來這裡做什麼？」弟弟說：「我想效法哥哥，齋戒沐浴，在這裡日夜殷勤祈禱，祈求天神保佑，讓我們兄弟兩人發財。」

instead. Maybe with the two of us praying, the Heavenly God would hear us and help both of us become rich faster," Lucas said.

Annoyed, Ian said, "We had an agreement! You were supposed to cultivate the field. It's a crucial[11] time now, the field needs water and fertilizer[12]! Otherwise, how will we have a good harvest in a couple of months?"

Still disguised as Lucas, the Heavenly God asked, "Must we do the planting, watering, and fertilizing for a fruitful harvest[13]?"

"Yes, of course! I thought you knew that!" Ian exclaimed.

"My dear brother, what kind of seeds have you planted?" Lucas asked.

Ian was stunned[14] into silence.

The Heavenly God transformed[15] himself back to his true form, and said to Ian, "I am the Heavenly God you've been praying to day and night. You must know that although others can support you to gain wealth and honor, you must do the hard work yourself. Do you know

VOCABULARY

11. crucial (adj.) 重要的
12. fertilizer (n.) 肥料
13. harvest (n.) 收穫期；收成
14. stunned (v.) 使驚嚇
15. transformed (v.) 轉換；變換

　　哥哥聽了很生氣，說：「你不去耕地、播種、澆水、鋤草、施肥，又怎能期待農作物會有收成呢？」

　　於是化身為弟弟的天神反問：「收成真的得要先播種嗎？那麼，哥哥你又播下什麼種子呢？」哥哥無言以對。

why you are so poor in this life?"

Ian shook his head, and replied softly, "I don't know..."

The Heavenly God continued, "In your past lives, you did not practice generosity[16], and you were stingy[17]. Therefore, you have only planted the seeds of stinginess. This is why you are poor in this life. Now, even though you diligently pray to me every day, you still reap the seeds, that is the causes and effects[18] of your past lives. In the same way, if you wish to harvest apples during the winter, praying to countless Heavenly Gods does not mean your wish will be granted[19]. You need to plant the seeds first to harvest the fruits later. Therefore, from today on, you should focus on practicing generosity. Only then will you be wealthy in the future."

Ian realized that it was pointless[20] to simply pray without any action. After that experience with the Heavenly God, he joined Lucas in

VOCABULARY

16. generosity (n.) 布施

17. stingy (adj.) 吝嗇的

18. causes and effects (n.) 因果

19. granted (v.) 給予；滿足

20. pointless (adj.) 無意義的

這時候，毗沙門天神回復原來的樣子，對哥哥說：「我就是你日夜祈求禮拜的毗沙門天神，我雖然可以給你助緣，但是想要獲得福德富貴，還是必須靠你自己去耕種。過去，你因為不肯布施，種下了慳吝的因，今生才會如此貧困，現在你雖然日夜精進禮拜我，但因果是無法違背的。就像要在冬天求得菴摩羅果一樣，縱然是禮拜百千天神，也是不可能的。所以，從今天起，你要修行布施，將來才能夠致富。」

cultivating their field. Later that year, they reaped a good harvest and shared it with the townspeople. The following year, the harvest was even better than the previous[21] one. With a continuous run of good harvests, Ian and Lucas were eventually[22] able to earn enough money to buy a new house.

This story highlights[23] that practicing generosity leads us to a path of wealth. However, most people think that giving only benefits[24] the one who receives[25] it.

VOCABULARY

21. previous (adj.) 先前的
22. eventually (adv.) 最終；終於
23. highlights (v.) 強調
24. benefits (v.) 使受益；受惠
25. receives (v.) 得到；收到

Also, how does giving bring wealth to the giver? Generosity is like planting seeds in a field. Once you have planted seeds, then you will surely have a harvest.

At the beginning of this story, Ian was not willing to put in the effort. Instead, he thought that simply praying would yield[26] good results. How often do we wish for something to happen without wanting to put in the effort to make it happen? With the help of the Heavenly God, he realized[27] that he must plant the right seeds to reap a good harvest. More importantly, sharing the harvest with others produced even better harvests in the following years.

Generosity does not only mean giving money. For example, we can speak good words, which is another form of generosity. Our words can deeply affect[28] others and so it is important that when talking with anyone, we do so with positivity[29] and encouragement[30]. Even if you do not know how to speak good words, you can offer others your strength. If you don't speak good words or have no strength to offer, it doesn't matter, because what is most important are your good intentions toward other people.

VOCABULARY

26. yield (v.) 產生；出產；得出
27. realized (v.) 意識到
28. affect (v.) 影響
29. positivity (n.) 正面；積極
30. encouragement (n.) 鼓勵；獎勵

布施是發財最好的方法，但一般人總以為布施是給人，既然給人，自己怎麼會發財？其實，布施好比在田地裡面播種，有播種才有收成。

Good intentions[31] are another form of generosity. When you see others speaking good words, or doing good deeds, you can rejoice[32] and feel happy for them. This kind of generosity generates[33] good merits for the giver. Therefore, by having a joyous[34] heart and mind, we can practice generosity in our daily lives[35].

VOCABULARY

31. intentions (n.) 目的；意圖

32. rejoice (v.) 非常高興；深感欣喜

33. generates (v.) 造成；引起

34. joyous (adj.) 高興的；歡快的

35. daily lives (n.) 日常生活

布施也不一定都是用金錢來布施，比方我們會說好話，說好話就是布施；你說我不會說好話，出力也是布施；或許你說我不會說好話，也沒有餘力，那也沒有關係，有心也能布施，聽到人家說好話、見到人家做好事，你心裡歡喜，隨喜也同樣有功德。大家不妨多布施自己的一念歡喜心吧！

Dharma Words by Venerable Master Hsing Yun

Generosity leads to a rich life,
while stinginess leads to a poor life.

星雲大師法語

懂得付出，不計較吃虧，
才是富有的人生。
錙銖必較，只知道接受，
必是貧窮的人生。

notes

17

On Generosity

The Queen's Ring

皇后的戒指

Bodhi Light Tales
73-The Queen's Ring

Once upon a time, there lived in India King Prasenajit. One day, while having a meal, he said to his wife, Mallika, "My Queen, you are loved and respected by the people. Everything good that has ever happened to you is because of me. If it weren't for me, you would not have what you have now, including your crown, jewelry, and everything else."

Hearing this, Queen Mallika replied, "Your majesty, it is actually due to many causes and conditions that we are husband and wife in this life."

Annoyed, the King said, "What causes and conditions? Nonsense[1], it's only because I'm King."

"My dear King, do you remember how we met?" the Queen asked.

"Yes of course! I remember it was right after my defeat[2] in battle with King Ajatashastru. On my way back, I was feeling miserable[3]. Then you appeared. I was enchanted[4] by your beautiful singing voice. When I saw you, your beauty dazzled[5] me. When I asked if you were married, I was so happy when you told me you were not.

---

1. nonsense (n.) 胡說
2. defeat (n.) 落敗；戰敗
3. miserable (adj.) 痛苦的
4. enchanted (v.) 著迷了
5. dazzled (v.) 使目眩；使傾倒

從前印度有個波斯匿王，有一天在吃飯的時候，他對皇后說：「妳現在身為一國之母，受到千萬民眾的愛戴與尊重，完全因為我是國王。假如沒有我，妳頭上戴的珠冠、身上披的瓔珞衣裳，以及所擁有的一切都會失去呀！」

I remember how comfortable I felt around you, and so I confided[6] in you about my defeat. You consoled[7] me with kind words and care. I knew then I wanted to bring you home," the King said.

"My dear king, what if that day, I had decided not to sing? What if you had thought my words were unkind? Do you think you would have taken me home then?"

The King thought for a while and quietly said, "Probably not."

The Queen continued, "Many causes and conditions came together for our encounter. Such causes and conditions are mutual[8] and harmonized[9]. That means you rely on me, and I rely on you. Therefore, my honor[10] and merit have come about because of you and me, not only because of you alone."

"If I'm not King, You would not be Queen," exclaimed the King.

"Even if I am not Queen, I will have my own merit and

VOCABULARY

6. confided (v.) 傾訴
7. consoled (v.) 安慰
8. mutual (adj.) 相互的
9. harmonized (adj.) 協調的
10. honor (n.) 尊敬；名譽

皇后一聽，她不以為然地說：「王啊！你我今生成為夫妻，都是因緣結合的，既是眾緣所成，就是你依於我、我依於你，因緣是相互依存的。因此，我的榮耀、我的福報來自於你，也來自於我，不完全是你賜給我的啊！」

virtue[11]," the Queen replied.

Feeling unappreciated[12] and belittled[13] by his wife, the King was furious, "If I never crowned you Queen, do you think people would respect you? Your merit and virtue come from me!"

The King's ego was hurt and he was outraged[14].

He saw the ring on the Queen's finger and said to his minister, "Remove the Queen's ring at once! Throw it into the river. I never want to see it again!"

He turned to the Queen and said, "Since you do not appreciate what I have given you, I shall take all that I have given you back!"

The Queen kept silent as she knew the King was too angry to listen to anything she had to say.

After their argument, the Queen reflected on their conversation. She recalled the Buddha's teachings and how she resolved[15] to practice compassion and patience. She did not feel angry towards the King. Every day, she continued to

---

VOCABULARY

11. virtue (n.) 德行；美德
12. unappreciated (v.) 不被賞識
13. belittled (v.) 輕視
14. outraged (adj.) 憤怒的
15. resolved (v.) 下定決心

國王一聽，非常生氣，認為皇后藐視他的威權，立刻要人取下皇后手上配戴的珠寶戒指，並且派人把它丟棄到汪洋大海裡。這時，國王趾高氣揚地對皇后說：「妳說妳的福報是妳自己的，現在妳手上擁有的戒指呢？」皇后默然不語。

do her daily Buddhist practices[16] as well as her duties as a wife.

A week passed and the King was still angry with his Queen. The Queen decided to ask the chef to cook the King's favorite dishes[17]. Knowing that the King liked to eat fish, the chef thought to prepare a big fish he recently[18] caught. When he cut open the fish, something dropped to the ground. As he picked it up, he saw that it was a ring.

He thought, "Why would there be a ring inside a fish?"

After preparing the dishes, the chef reported the ring to the minister. Upon seeing the ring, the minister kept quiet, grabbed[19] the ring, and went to see the King.

Both the King and Queen were already seated at the table, ready for their meal.

The Queen smiled and said, "My dear King, I'm grateful[20] for everything you have done for me. So everything here has been prepared especially for you."

VOCABULARY

16. practices (n.) 實踐
17. dishes (n.) 菜餚
18. recently (adv.) 最近；近來
19. grabbed (v.) 抓取
20. grateful (adj.) 感激的

有一天，御廚在烹煮一條大魚的時候，魚肚子一剖開，竟然出現了一枚戒指。這究竟是怎麼回事呢？原來戒指才被丟進海裡，就遇上一條飢餓的大魚，一口便將它吃下肚去了。後來這條大魚被漁人捕獲，也輾轉呈獻到了皇宮裡。

The King, now happier, smiled and nodded.

At that moment, the minister came forward and presented[21] the ring to the King. When everyone saw the ring, they all recognized[22] it as the Queen's ring.

The minister explained to his King, "Your majesty, this ring was found inside the big fish being served today. It appears that the ring you had ordered to be thrown in the river was swallowed[23] by this fish. After the fish was caught, it was brought to the palace to be made ready for your special meal."

Astonished[24], the King finally understood what the Queen meant about causes and conditions coming together. He then returned the ring to his Queen.

She happily put the ring back on and said smugly[25], "Whatever is meant to be mine will still be mine." They both laughed and began eating.

After this experience, King

VOCABULARY

21. presented (v.) 提交
22. recognized (v.) 認出
23. swallowed (v.) 吞下
24. astonished (adj.) 感到震驚的
25. smugly (adv.) 得意地

大家一看到這枚戒指，即刻認出那是皇后所有，立刻就將它交還給了皇后。皇后戴著失而復得的戒指，歡喜地對波斯匿王說：「你看吧！該是我的，它終究會是我的。」

Prasenajit realized that every person has their own merit. It cannot be taken away by anyone. For every action, there is a consequence[26].

This story draws on the proverb[27], "We reap what we sow." In other words, depending on how much we have sowed, it is what we can expect to harvest. But, we must also understand the concept of causes and conditions. Everything in this world arises depending on[28] other conditions, and nothing is possible without existing in a web of causes and conditions.

For example, let us take a seed of a flower. The seed is the cause and the flower is the effect. Between that seed being planted and becoming a flower, many conditions are required. These conditions are water, soil, air, sunlight, and so on. Without any of these elements[29], the seed will not be able to grow into a flower. Therefore, we can also see that the seed coexists[30] with the required conditions, and there is a mutual relationship between them.

This concept can also be applied to this story. The relationship between King Prasenajit and Queen Mallika is one of coexistence. They rely on each

---

VOCABULARY

26. consequence (n.) 結果；後果
27. proverb (n.) 諺語
28. depending on (phrase) 取決於……
29. elements (n.) 要素
30. coexists (v.) 共生；共處；共存

波斯匿王經過這樣的事情後，從此深信，一個人的窮通禍福不是別人所能左右的，各人有各人的福報，一個人過去播種幾分，現在收穫就有幾分。

other, and there are many causes and conditions for the relationship to work. Though it may be true that without the King's decision to crown Mallika as Queen, her life would be very different. On the other hand, the Queen's virtues and merits were due to her efforts in practicing generosity, compassion, and patience. Her ring coming back to her through being swallowed by a fish represents her merits. As the saying goes, "Life's disasters and fortunes are incurred[31] by one's actions." Ultimately[32], we are in charge of our destiny based on the merits that we accumulate[33].

VOCABULARY

31. incurred (v.) 招致
32. ultimately (adv.) 最終；最後
33. accumulate (v.) 積累；積聚

Dharma Words by Venerable Master Hsing Yun

Good or bad fruit comes from good or bad causes and conditions;
You are your own gardener.
Good or bad karmic justice comes from good or ill will;
You are the master of your own will.

星雲大師法語

種善因得善果，種惡因得惡果，
人是自己的園丁。
存好心得好報，存歹心得歹報，
心是自己的主人。

notes

18

On Generosity

Heaven and Hell

天堂地獄的筷子

Once upon a time, there lived a writer named Edward. He worked for a magazine featuring[1] a wide range of topics about people, cultures, traditions, and philosophy[2]. His latest task was to write a piece about heaven and hell. Though he was always a curious[3] person, he had never really thought about heaven and hell.

One evening, Edward was having dinner with Ellie, his girlfriend. While waiting for their food, Ellie said, "Is something bothering[4] you?"

"Nothing's bothering me..." Edward replied.

"Come on, I know when something's on your mind. Is it work?" Ellie asked.

"Maybe..." Edward replied.

"What must you write about this time?" Ellie asked.

"Hmm...I need to write about heaven and hell. I don't know...I've never thought about it. I don't know where to begin," Edward replied.

"Heaven and hell...That sounds interesting! I've always heard people say, 'If you do bad things, then you are bound[5] to be reborn in

VOCABULARY

1. featuring (v.) 以…特寫
2. philosophy (n.) 哲學
3. curious (adj.) 好奇的
4. bothering (v.) 煩擾
5. bound (adj.) 肯定的；極有可能的

有一個人經常聽人說做壞事要墮地獄受苦，做善事能生天堂享福，但是天堂、地獄是什麼樣子，他並不知道。一個偶然的因緣，他遇到一個修道人。修道人對他說：「我可以帶你到天堂和地獄去參觀！」聽聞此話，這個人很高興地就答應了。

hell to bear the consequences[6]. If you do good things, then you'll be reborn in heaven to enjoy yourself,'" Ellie said.

"Sounds like angels and demons to me," Edward replied.

"Yes, it does. I'm not sure if heaven or hell do exist. I think it's best you do some research[7] on it," Ellie said.

"Yes, for sure, I need to research and see what I can find. I don't think I can write about something so unknown to me. It does make me wonder[8] exactly what heaven and hell are like?" Edward said.

"Well, I'm sure you'll find something to inspire[9] you, like always. You're good at what you do," Ellie replied.

"Thanks! But let's not talk about work anymore," Edward replied just as the waiter arrived with their main course[10].

On their way home, Edward thought about

VOCABULARY

6. consequences (n.) 結果；後果
7. research (n.) 研究；調查
8. wonder (v.) 疑惑；想知道
9. inspire (v.) 賦予靈感
10. main course (n.) 主菜

what Ellie said about being reborn in heaven and hell due to one's actions. He tried to picture what heaven and hell could be like, but it proved[11] difficult since he'd never thought about it.

That night, Edward had a dream. In his dream, he met a man named Michael, who said to him, "I can take you on a tour[12] of heaven and hell, would you like that?"

"Wow! How did you know that...?" Edward replied.

"Is that a yes?" Michael asked.

"Yes, of course. I would love to visit both places!" Edward said excitedly[13].

Michael told Edward to close his eyes, and lifted[14] him in the air. When Edward opened his eyes, he was in hell. Looking around, Edward whispered[15] to Michael, "People here look exactly like people do on Earth. They seem like they need to eat and sleep just like we do."

Michael smiled and pointing to his left, said,

---

11. proved (v.) 證明是；結果是
12. tour (n.) 參觀；觀光
13. excitedly (adv.) 興奮地
14. lifted (v.) 舉起；抬起
15. whispered (v.) 低聲說

首先，他隨著修道人來到地獄。初來乍到，他發現地獄和人間的生活差不多，一樣要穿衣、吃飯、睡覺，只有一點不同，就是地獄裡的人吃飯，所使用的筷子有三尺長，每當有人夾起菜肴要往嘴裡送的時候，從左邊送，就被左邊的人給搶去；從右邊送，就被右邊的人給搶去，自己永遠都吃不到。也因此，彼此都在怨怪：「你偷吃了我的菜！」「他搶去了我的菜！」爭吵不休，不得安寧。

"Take a look at them."

Edward saw people holding forks, but each fork was over a foot in length. Each time someone picked up food with their fork, before the food could reach their mouths, it would be snatched[16] and eaten by other people. Regardless[17] of how many times a person tried to grab food with their fork, someone would snatch the food and eat it. Since no one would let anyone else have food, nobody could quench[18] their hunger. Worse still, they blamed[19] each other. Someone would say, "You stole my food!" Another would reply, "They stole mine!" On and on, they kept arguing. There was no peace whatsoever.

Edward sighed[20] and felt deeply sorry for these people in hell.

Then, Michael said, "How about we go to heaven now?"

Edward nodded.

Michael told Edward to cover his eyes again, and lifted him in the air. When Edward opened his eyes, he found himself in heaven. Right away,

VOCABULARY

16. snatched (v.) 搶奪;攫取
17. regardless (adv.)
    不管怎樣;無論如何
18. quench (v.) 滿足
19. blamed (v.) 責備;責怪
20. sighed (v.) 歎息;歎氣

he felt a sense of calm[21] and peace. He looked around.

Michael pointed down and said, "Look there."

Edward noticed again that the people here were no different from people on Earth, they needed to eat and sleep as well. However, there was something different about them compared to the people in hell.

Edward said to Michael, "The people here also use forks that are a foot long. But the difference is, when they pick up food with their fork, instead of eating the food themselves, they offer it to the people in front of them. They feed each other. This is so nice, everyone is polite[22] and willing to help each other. They even thank each other for being kind. Unlike hell, people here live happily together and in harmony[23]."

Michael then tapped[24] Edward on the shoulder...and suddenly Edward was woken up by Ellie tapping him on the shoulder, whispering[25], "Edward, wake up...Are you all right?"

VOCABULARY

21. calm (n.) 平靜
22. polite (adj.) 有禮貌的
23. harmony (n.) 和諧；融洽
24. tapped (v.) 輕拍
25. whispering (v.) 耳語

接著，修道人又帶他到天堂裡。天堂和人間的生活也是一樣，要穿衣、吃飯、工作，甚至吃飯用的筷子和地獄相同，也是三尺長，唯一不同的是，他們夾了菜，不是朝自己的嘴裡送，而是給你吃、給他吃。如此一來，彼此都在互道感謝，相處非常和樂。

Edward groaned[26] as he opened his eyes, and muttered[27], "What happened?"

"I heard you mumbling[28] and talking in your sleep. So I thought I'd better wake you up." Ellie said.

Edward realized that everything he experienced with Michael was a dream. Sitting by the side of the bed, he now tried to make sense of what he had dreamed.

"I'll go make breakfast," Ellie said and then left the room.

Edward picked up his notebook and began writing down everything he had seen in his dream.

After a couple of months of research and drawing inspiration[29] from his dream, Edward finished the article on heaven and hell. Many readers of the magazine responded with questions that sparked[30] lively discussions on the topic.

VOCABULARY

26. groaned (v.) 呻吟；嘆息
27. muttered (v.) 喃喃低語
28. mumbling (v.) 喃喃而語；咕噥
29. inspiration (n.) 靈感
30. sparked (v.) 引起；觸發

　　從這一段譬喻就可以知道，什麼是天堂？能把歡喜給人、把福利給人，大家互相讚美、尊重，就是天堂。什麼是地獄？不重視大眾，不顧念他人，不為別人設想，自私自利，就是地獄。

This story illustrates the contrast between heaven and hell. If we bring joy to others, benefit them, as well as praise[31] and respect each other, then heaven is where we are.

On the other hand, if we are selfish, thinking only about ourselves and never paying attention[32] to others, not caring about them, and looking only to our benefit, then we are already in hell. Like this story, people in hell think only of themselves, so no one is happy.

It is important to remember that heaven and hell are not fixed[33] places we journey to. They already exist in our minds. Every day, each one of us has kind thoughts[34] and bad thoughts. When we have kind thoughts, everyone seems nice and we are happy. When we have bad thoughts, everyone seems like an enemy[35] and we are unhappy. In other words, once we have kind thoughts, we are in heaven. Once we have bad thoughts, we are in hell. Therefore, we all go through heaven and hell several times each day.

The key question we should ask ourselves daily is, do I choose to be in heaven or hell?

VOCABULARY

31. praise (v.) 讚揚；表揚
32. attention (n.) 注意；留心
33. fixed (adj.) 固定的
34. thoughts (n.) 思想；念頭
35. enemy (n.) 敵人；仇敵

因此，天堂、地獄不在他方，就在我們自己的心中。可以說，每一個人一天當中，在天堂、地獄裡來回好多次，一念善心起，就是天堂，一念惡心起，地獄即現前。自己不妨可以想一想，我究竟是上天堂多呢？還是下地獄多呢？

Dharma Words by Venerable Master Hsing Yun

Defilement and ignorance bring you hell,
while enlightenment and right understanding bring you heaven.
Sorrow and trouble bring you hell,
while peace and joy bring you heaven.

星雲大師法語

心中煩惱無明即地獄，心中菩提正見即天堂，
心中憂悲苦惱即地獄，心中安樂幸福即天堂。

notes

19

On Generosity

A Generous Donation

銀貨兩訖

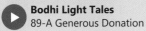

Bodhi Light Tales
89-A Generous Donation

Scan me to listen!

掃我，聆聽故事！

Once upon a time, there lived a Chan Master named Tanyi. He lived in a monastery inherited[1] from his master. The monastery was old and some areas were in urgent[2] need of repair, so the Chan Master decided it was time to renovate[3] the monastery.

One day, a volunteer named Jeff came to the monastery bringing his fresh vegetables.

When he arrived at the kitchen, the Chef said, "Good to see you, Jeff! I see you brought us more veggies."

Jeff smiled and said, "Yes, freshly picked from the field this morning."

The Chef said, "We're really lucky to have your fresh vegetables. You're a true gentleman! Thank you so much. We are eternally[4] grateful!"

"Please, don't mention it[5]. It's nothing. Besides, I am happy to practice generosity, just as taught by the Buddha," Jeff replied. He was so pleased to have been praised by the Chef that he stayed around to help.

While preparing lunch, Jeff overheard a

VOCABULARY

1. inherited (v.) 繼承
2. urgent (adj.) 緊急的；急迫的
3. renovate (v.) 修復
4. eternally (adv.) 永遠地
5. don't mention it (phrase) 不客氣；不用謝

　　曇一禪師要想修建一座寺院，有一位信徒聽到消息，立刻就捐了五十兩銀子，並且得意地對禪師說：「禪師，我捐給你五十兩銀子喔！」禪師聽後，只是輕輕點頭應諾，收下銀子，便轉身去忙其他的事。

conversation about the ongoing renovation of the monastery. He thought to himself, "This renovation means the monastery will need a lot of money, maybe I should contribute[6]." Jeff continued to help in the kitchen, but the thought of contributing to the renovation continued to linger[7] in his mind all day.

The next morning, Jeff came to the monastery and asked to see the Chan Master. When he saw the Chan Master, he said, "Master, I heard you wish to repair the monastery, and I'd like to offer my support. Please kindly accept my donation," he then gave an envelope to the Chan Master.

The Chan Master took the envelope and said, "Thank you."

After a moment of awkward[8] silence, Jeff continued, "Master, the Buddha taught that we should practice generosity. Since the monastery will need funds[9] to be restored[10], I feel like I should do my part."

The Chan Master said, "I understand." Then,

VOCABULARY

6. contribute (v.) 出力；捐獻
7. linger (v.) 徘徊
8. awkward (adj.) 尷尬的
9. funds (n.) 資金
10. restored (v.) 修復；重建

信徒覺得很奇怪，五十兩銀子不是小數目，怎麼交給了禪師，他卻連一聲「謝謝」都沒有呢？不過，信徒又想，大概是曇一禪師沒有聽清楚我說的話，不知道這是五十兩銀子。所以，隨後他又大聲地說：「禪師，那是五十兩的銀子呀！」

he raised his cup of tea and said to Jeff, "Please have some tea."

"Thank you," Jeff said.

The Chan Master and Jeff then sat in silence for some time.

As the uncomfortable[11] silence grew longer, Jeff thought, "Why did the Master simply say thank you? Maybe he didn't understand me, or maybe he doesn't know how much money I'm giving?"

So, he spoke up, "Master, inside the envelope is five thousand dollars. I've worked hard to earn it but I give it to you."

The Chan Master nodded and replied, "I am sure you worked hard for that money."

Suddenly, their conversation[12] was interrupted[13] by the phone ringing.

While the Chan Master answered the phone, Jeff thought, "Is five thousand dollars too little? Why doesn't the Chan Master show his appreciation[14] instead of simply saying thank you? Even the Chef praised[15] me more

VOCABULARY

11. uncomfortable (adj.) 不舒服的
12. conversation (n.) 交談；對話
13. interrupted (v.) 中斷
14. appreciation (n.) 感激
15. praised (v.) 讚美；稱讚

曇一禪師聽了仍是淡淡地說：「哦！哦！哦！」也沒有表示什麼意思，就往佛殿的方向走去了。信徒看禪師冷漠的樣子，心裡很不高興：我們在家人賺錢很不容易，我捐給你五十兩銀子，你怎麼連一聲「謝謝」也沒有，就不能表示一點重視的樣子嗎？

這位信徒繼續跟著禪師走向佛殿，路上終於忍耐不住，說：「禪師，剛才給你的五十兩銀子，難道沒有價值嗎？」

for bringing vegetables?!"

When the Master finished with his phone call, Jeff spoke up, "Master, does my donation mean nothing to you?

"Why would you think that?" the Chan Master asked.

"Because you simply said thank you," Jeff replied unhappily.

The Chan Master nodded and said, "I see... Please come with me."

Jeff reluctantly[16] got up and followed the Chan Master.

Arriving at the Main Shrine, the Chan Master prostrated[17] to the Buddha statue. With joined palms, he said, "Oh Great Compassionate Buddha, this devotee just donated five thousand dollars to the monastery. Before you, I would like to acknowledge[18] him and offer him our sincere gratitude[19]."

The Chan Master turned to Jeff and said, "Thank you very much! We are ever grateful for your generous[20] donation, not only of money

16. reluctantly (adv.) 不情願地
17. prostrated (v.) 禮拜
18. acknowledge (v.) 感激；答謝
19. gratitude (n.) 感激之情；感謝
20. generous (adj.) 慷慨的；大方的

這時候，曇一禪師已經走到了佛殿前，聽到信徒這句話，趕緊停下來，回應道：「哦！哦！」接著就對著佛殿裡的佛祖大聲說：「佛祖啊！這一位信徒捐給寺院五十兩銀子，現在我就代表佛祖向他說一聲：『謝謝！謝謝！』」說罷，曇一禪師繼續又說：「這樣總可以『銀貨兩訖』了吧？」

but also of food and more importantly, your time and efforts. May the Buddha bless you for all that you do for the monastery, whether it be gifting us vegetables, money, or helping in any way that you can."

Now embarrassed[21], Jeff joined his palms and bowed. He thought, "Why was I so greedy in expecting more than a sincere thank you? Why did I think that simply because I donated money I deserved to be unduly[22] praised? I must realize that I must also be grateful for the causes and conditions[23] that enable me to give. From now on, I shall learn to give without expecting anything in return."

This story teaches us the true meaning of generosity. Jeff's generosity was without a doubt[24] valuable. However, his intentions[25] when making that donation were partly driven by his wish for the Chan Master to acknowledge him and publicly show his appreciation. Many people, in return for their generosity, wish for their names to be carved on a wall or recorded in books. If the act of giving is not publicly

VOCABULARY

21. embarrassed (adj.) 尷尬的；不好意思的
22. unduly (adv.) 過度地
23. causes and conditions (phrase) 因緣
24. doubt (n.) 懷疑
25. intentions (n.) 目的；意圖

信徒聽了，感到很慚愧，心想：難道我奉獻給佛祖，一定得貪求一聲「謝謝」，立一個功德芳名，留一個紀錄，才能補償自己這五十兩銀子的奉獻嗎？

acknowledged or appreciated, is it of any lesser value?

The reality is, if we do good deeds in search of recognition, then the worth of our generosity is already devalued. If we selfishly seek only acknowledgment[26] and praise, our merits are lessened.

On the other hand, if we give with a mindset of sincerity and pure intention, devoid[27] of greed, then our merits and virtues are unlimited. Jeff was upset that he had received no public acknowledgment in return for his donation. When we can recognize that true giving is selfless, our generosity becomes immeasurable[28].

As a devotee, we have the responsibility to protect, support, and contribute to our faith. However, it is as important to have a mindset of expecting nothing in return. There is a saying, "The meaning of life is to find your gift, while the purpose of life is to give it away." Through giving without greed or attachment[29], our merits and virtues are elevated[30].

The Buddha reminds us that when we give, our state of mind must be one of joy before, during, and

---

VOCABULARY

26. acknowledgment (n.) 感謝
27. devoid (adj.) 全無的
28. immeasurable (adj.) 無限的
29. attachment (n.) 執著
30. elevated (v.) 提昇;提高

其實,這種有相的施捨,反而把布施的價值及功德減低了,假如是無相的施捨,冥冥中自有功德福報,何必要計較呢?

希望每一個宗教的信徒,對宗教的擁護、對宗教的支持、對宗教的奉獻,都能帶著一種無償的心理,不要有「銀貨兩訖」的心態。所謂「有心栽花花不開,無意插柳柳成蔭」,無相布施的功德才大,有相布施的功德反而少啊!

after the act. This means that when we give, we do so with happiness, and after we have given, we let go[31] of our selfish desires[32].

VOCABULARY

31. let go (v.) 放下
32. desires (n.) 欲望

Dharma Words by Venerable Master Hsing Yun

Only the poor want more;
Only the wealthy give joyously.

星雲大師法語

多求的原因是貧窮，
喜捨的結果會富有。

notes

20

On Generosity

Offering a Bun

羅漢與包子

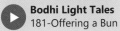

Bodhi Light Tales
181-Offering a Bun

Scan me to listen!
掃我，聆聽故事!

Once upon a time, there lived a disciple of Buddha named Ajita. He was one of the eighteen arhats, known as the "arhat with long eyebrows." Ajita was revered[1] for his supernatural powers[2] and limitless[3] spiritual abilities. According to Buddhist texts, he still lives in the world today, possibly over 2600 years old.

Ajita was a wise and compassionate monk who lived a simple life, following Buddha's teachings closely. He spent his days meditating and helping others whenever he could. He believed that every person had the potential[4] to attain enlightenment and live a life of happiness and contentment.

One day, Ajita went out to beg for alms in a nearby village, as was the custom of monks in ancient India. He walked through the streets with his alms bowl, hoping to receive some food from the kind-hearted[5] people of the village. As he walked, he came across a food stall where a

VOCABULARY

1. revered (v.) 尊敬；崇敬
2. supernatural powers (n.) 神通
3. limitless (adj.) 無限的
4. potential (n.) 潛力；潛能
5. kind-hearted (adj.) 好心腸的；熱心的

在十八羅漢當中，有一位羅漢眉毛很長，被稱為「長眉羅漢」。長眉羅漢神通廣大，法力無邊，根據經典記載，他現在還活在世間，算一算歲數，應該也有二千六百多歲了。

有一天，長眉羅漢出外托缽乞食，在街頭碰到一個婦人賣包子，便站到了她的身旁，想向她化緣。賣包子的婦人看了，心裡很不高興，作勢要將他趕走，並且說：「喂！出家人站旁邊去，不要妨礙我做生意！」長眉羅漢於是走到一旁，就地坐了下來，雙眼一閉就入定了。

woman was selling buns. The woman selling the buns saw Ajita but pretended[6] to be busy and ignored[7] him. Ajita stepped forward to make sure the woman noticed him, but she responded unhappily, "Hey, monk! Don't stand in front of my stall; you're blocking my business. Go stand over there."

Without saying a word, Ajita joined his palms, stepped aside, and sat down, closing his eyes to meditate. Seeing this, the woman became worried, thinking to herself, "What's happening here? He seems not to be moving at all; what if he dies here? I'll be in trouble with the authorities[8]!" In a panic, she yelled, "Hey! Wake up, wake up! I'll give you a bun!"

Upon hearing this, Ajita immediately[9] opened his eyes and stood up.

The woman, seeing that Ajita was perfectly fine, changed her mind and thought, "Do I have to give him a bun? I really don't want to!" Then she had an idea and silently muttered[10] to herself, "I know! I'll just make a smaller bun! The

婦人見狀，不知道這是打坐入定，直呼：「不得了了，萬一他死在這裡怎麼辦？會給官員治罪啊！」心裡一慌張，趕快就說：「喂！你醒來吧、你醒來吧，我願意給你一顆包子！」長眉羅漢聽到婦人的話，立刻睜開眼睛，站了起來。

眼見長眉羅漢好端端的樣子，婦人倒是不甘願了，心裡想：我偏不要給你大包子，弄個水餃大小的小

size of a dumpling will be perfect!"

Ajita, who knew exactly what the woman was thinking, decided to use his powers to teach her a lesson. As the woman prepared the small bun, he made sure it stuck[11] to the bigger buns on the left and right. When the woman saw that the small bun was sticking to the bigger buns next to it, she tried to separate them, becoming more and more anxious[12]. She pulled and stretched the buns with all her might but could not separate them. Feeling exhausted, the woman sighed and said, "All right, fine! You can have all of these!"

Ajita smiled and nodded, happily receiving the buns. As he was about to leave, he said, "Madam, I am a monk who has attained the fruit of arhatship[13]. Even if I do not eat, I will not starve to death. I have supernatural powers that can help me sustain[14] my body and feast on the joy of meditation[15]. However, some of my fellow monks are not in good health. They are unable to leave the monastery to beg for alms,

---

包子給你就好!長眉羅漢知道她的心意,就施展了一個小小的神通法力,讓婦人做的小包子,一下子黏到左邊的大包子,一下子又碰到右邊的大包子。

婦人看到這樣的情況,心裡很著急,雙手使勁地要把大小包子分離,但是不論她怎麼使力,都無法分開。到最後,婦人已經筋疲力盡,就說:「唉!算了、算了!包子統統給你吧!」

so I will bring these buns back to them. Once they regain their energy, they can continue their spiritual practice. On their behalf, I thank you."

Upon hearing this, the woman was moved and said joyfully, "Since that's the case, let me give you some more buns!" She packed all her remaining buns and, with her palms joined, said, "Please accept my offering. I am very sorry for being rude to you earlier."

Ajita graciously[16] accepted the woman's offering and thanked her, saying, "Thank you so much. By making an offering with a joyful heart, you have accumulated[17] great merit and virtues[18] that will bring you blessings in the future."

The news of the woman's act of generosity spread quickly throughout the village, and many people were inspired[19] by her example. They began to give with a joyful heart, and soon the whole community was transformed[20]. People who used to be selfish and greedy began to share their wealth with those in need, and the

VOCABULARY

16. graciously (adv.) 有禮貌地
17. accumulated (v.) 積累；積聚
18. merit and virtues (n.) 福德
19. inspired (adj.) 得到靈感的
20. transformed (adj.) 轉化的

長眉羅漢開心地拿了包子就要走，臨走前，他說：「婦人家，我是個證果的阿羅漢，就算我不吃飯也不會餓死，我有神通法力，能以禪悅為食，只是我的同道們身體不好，不能出來托缽化緣，所以只好由我帶幾個包子回去給他們吃，他們氣力充足了，就可以安心辦道。」婦人一聽，受到感動，心生歡喜，就說：「既然是這樣，那我就多送幾個包子給你吧！」

village became known for its spirit of generosity and kindness.

Years passed, and the woman grew old and eventually passed away. It was said that she had accumulated so many merits from her joyful giving that she was reborn in heaven, surrounded by the fruits of her good deeds. Her descendants[21] prospered[22], and the village continued to thrive[23].

This story highlights the significance of "joyful giving.[24]" When one gives with a joyful heart, they cultivate a positive attitude and generate positive energy. This can lead to a sense of satisfaction and fulfillment, inspiring others to give and creating a positive cycle of generosity and goodwill[25]. Giving with a joyful heart can increase one's blessings and merits. Therefore, those who practice joyful giving are considered to be the wealthiest people in the world. The more one practices joyful giving, the more one is blessed with merits.

VOCABULARY

21. descendants (n.) 後裔；子孫
22. prospered (v.) 使成功；使昌盛
23. thrive (v.) 繁榮；興旺
24. joyful giving (n.) 歡喜布施
25. goodwill (n.) 善意；友善

長眉羅漢接受了婦人供養的包子，離開時，向他道謝說：「婦人家，妳用歡喜心把東西布施給人，將來會有大功德！」後來，這個婦人家果然因為當初的歡喜布施，而生到天上享受天福了。

佛教講究「喜捨」，歡喜布施能增加福德，一個人越是喜捨，就越有福報。所以，時時懷著歡喜心布施結緣的人，是世界上最富有的人。

Dharma Words by Venerable Master Hsing Yun

Greed cannot make fortune.
Joyful giving can bring many blessings.
Be modest when benefiting others.
Modesty helps liberate sentient beings.

星雲大師法語

貪心不能致富，
喜捨才能多福，
利他不忘自謙，
自謙才能度眾。

notes

notes

notes

Credits 致謝

The Bodhi Light Tales were initially published on the Bodhi Light Tales Anchor podcast channel. We would like to express our heartfelt gratitude to everyone for their dedicated efforts.

《星雲說喻》最初以有聲書形式於 Anchor 播客平台推出，為「菩提心燈」系列故事。今結集成冊，特此感謝製作團隊的付出。

Editor-in-Chief 主編:
Venerable Miao Guang 妙光法師

Project Manager 專案執行:
Venerable Zhi Sheng 知笙法師

English Translators 英文翻譯:
Venerable Zhi Sheng 知笙法師
Belinda Hsueh 薛瑋瑩
Angela Ho 何慧玲

English Editors 英文編輯:
Arthur van Sevendonck
Jennifer Hsu 許嫡娟
Neil Lee
Jenny Liu

Vocabulary Assistants 中英詞彙表整理:
Kathryn Lee 李苑嫣
Belinda Hsueh 薛瑋瑩
Handayani Fu

English Story Proofreaders 英文故事校稿:
Venerable Zhi Mu 知睦法師
Arthur van Sevendonck
Huang Hsin-yu 黃馨玉
Kathryn Lee 李苑嫣
Annie Lam 藍安妮

Logo & Graphic Designer 平面設計:
Sedona Garcia

Illustrators (In order of illustrations contributed)
繪圖 (按圖次序):
Venerable Dao Pu 道璞法師
Venerable Neng Hui 能輝法師
Jack Yu 游智光
Lo Wan-ching 羅婉菁
Jonathon Cheung
Shi Jinhui 施金輝
Sedona Garcia
Venerable Zhi Yue 知悅法師
Zeng Jing-yi 曾靜怡
Valerie Tan

Podcast Audio Narrator 故事朗讀:
Venerable Miao Guang 妙光法師

Social Media Strategist 社群媒體策略:
Selene Chew 周思蕾

Podcast Intro & Outro Music Composer 音樂創作:
Nicholas Ng

Podcast Audio Editor 音檔剪輯:
Venerable Zhi Sheng 知笙法師

財團法人佛光山人間佛教研究院
Fo Guang Shan Institute of Humanistic Buddhism